# REMOTE
# TEAMS
# CONNECTED

*The Winning Strategy to Establish
a Profitable Team Work with the
Best Digital Tools and Have
Immediate Impact on Your Business*

## Matthew K. Atkins

Remote Teams Connected

Copyright © 2020 Matthew K. Atkins

Printed by Line Profile Ed.

First printing, June 2020.

Line Profile Ed.

https://www.lineprofile.net

# Table of Contents

# Preface

The commitment to learn new digital tools and manage your business remotely can be the opportunity to renew the mindset in your work team. Instead of passively experience the very real changes that are taking place in the world of remote working right now, this book will describe the best methods to benefit from the advantages of the digital world. We do it by establishing new values that can induce a profound transformation of the team's mission and objectives.

It's remarkable to think about how far the workforce has come and the tremendous leaps and bounds made over the years, especially where technology is concerned. We're now able to have virtual meetings with people across several continents at once through a range of available software to support this need. As incredible as it is, this experience can be frustrating when you don't have the right tools to support what you need to get done at the time. These frustrations and interruptions can lead to a loss of productivity and a lot of wasted time. With the changes in the way we communicate when working remotely, it also calls for a new set of behaviors and protocols to be put in place.

The same concept of leadership changes when you're coordinating a team of people who live far from each other, perhaps even on the other side of the world and across several continents. The world is such a globalized landscape these days, and companies have become more diverse today than they have ever been. A time like this calls for new strategies that can be used to reformulate the structure of traditional leadership, businesses and obtain unexpected benefits, such as:

- Saving money on travel and transfer expenses

- Saving money on office space rental and high overhead costs for the business.

- Improving the quality of life of team members

- Learning new IT solutions that increase productivity

- Getting results faster using more effective methods

- Having a competitive advantage as early adopters of the remote working life

- Work wherever you'll find an internet connection. Even work while you travel if you wanted.

In this book, you will find an organization survival kit that will help you prepare and track online meetings, manage and share documents, work together on the same document online. Gain insight into the remote working tips needed to improve ergonomics and better organize the workspace at home.

Finally, we will discuss the best techniques to feel fully involved in projects even more than before and, as a leader, to have full control of the business development and of its growth. Remote working is the future. When an employee's eyes have been opened to the possibility of what life could be like as a work from home staff, there's no going back. Once employers start to realize how much of a positive impact remote working has on the happiness and wellbeing of their staff, an employer who truly cares would be more than willing to consider letting their team members work from home to achieve that much-needed balance between work and personal life.

# Introduction

Congratulations on purchasing *Remote Teams Connected,* we hope you will benefit from the content of this book and you will implement many of the suggestions that we discuss below in your daily business.

A revolution is taking place right now. It's going on around us right now, at this very minute. But the revolution has been around for a while now, except that a lot of people never paid much attention to it because we're so used to the usual style of working. We wake up in the morning when the alarm buzzes, get dressed, head out the door, commute to the office, punch out at the end of the day, and commute back home. That has been the norm for as long as we can remember, and we never knew any other way to do it. That is until the Internet and technology opened the door to a whole new world of possibilities. The possibility of working remotely. *That* is the revolution that is happening right now. The working remotely revolution.

Think you've never heard of the remote working before? Well, that might be because you knew it by several other names. Telecommuting, for example. Or perhaps teleworker, which refers to a person who occasionally works from outside the office. Some businesses even employ people who get things done remotely without the need to ever step into the office. As long as they've got a good internet connection, a working computer, and any other tools they need to get the job done, they can work from anywhere in the world. They could be at the coffee shop next door, or perhaps halfway around the world. The possibilities are incredible with this revolutionary way of working.

The technology to work remotely has been around for a while, but it's probably only in 2020 that we started truly appreciating what these tools at our disposal could do. Ever since the year 2020, when many businesses globally were, in a way, obligated to resort to remote work because of the pandemic that took place, it turned out to be a good thing after all. It opened our eyes to the wondrous possibilities of what working from home can be like since people around the world have been forced to go into self-isolation at home, the option to work from home has always been here. We've just been far too comfortable with the "traditional" way of going to work that we never gave the idea the consideration it deserved.

This guide is going to change all of that. The ability to work from home is an opportunity in disguise. How? Let's explore the next few chapters to find out. This guide is suitable for anyone looking to learn how to efficiently manage and effectively lead a remote team. The digital opportunities out there are aplenty, and it takes a strong, capable, knowledgeable leader to power a remote team to success. Becoming a remote leader is an experience unlike any other, and this book is where you begin building the mindset needed for success. This is where you gain your inspiration as well as the tools you need to begin your leadership journey, and for those looking to discover the truth about what it's like to work from home? Well, we've got you covered too.

Among the other books on this subject, *Remote Teams Connected* is the guide committed to showing you the right way to build your remote working team efficiently. The digital world is the future, and businesses, managers, employees, and even freelancers everywhere can benefit from the techniques in this book. Make remote working simpler, faster, measurable, and achieve the results you want in a shorter amount of time while enjoying the freedom and flexibility of the work from home life. Why? Because your mental and physical well-being will thank you for it.

Every effort was made to ensure it is full of as much useful information as possible, please enjoy!

# Chapter 1

# A New Style of Working

Ask most employers, and they will probably tell you they believe an employee needs to be at an organization to be effective. In fact, if it weren't for the 2020 COVID-19 isolation and quarantine requirement that forced everyone to work from home as part of the social distancing and safety measures to help curb the spread of the highly contagious virus, it would be hard to shift away from this kind of mindset. It's perfectly understandable. It's hard to introduce change to a process that has been taking place ever since we can remember. Even the earliest humans had to leave their homes to go out and hunt, which was their way of working. For centuries people have been working hard the traditional way, and it was only after technology had been around for several years that companies and employers slowly started to change their minds about that.

**Is the Old Way of Commuting to Work That Bad?**

14

That depends on how you look at it. For those who live close by, commuting to work is not really a problem. But what about those that need to spend anywhere from an hour or more *one way* going to work? By the time they get through the traffic or the crowded public transportation system during rush hour, they're so stressed out when they arrive at work that they're not in the right headspace anymore to be productive, let alone engage positively with their colleagues or supervisors. Imagine experiencing that stressful commute on a daily basis? Is it any wonder there is a reduction in productivity in office spaces?

Now, compare that to the remote working employee. They don't have to wake up as early anymore because they don't have to make the long commute and spend all that time getting ready for work. They don't feel as stressed since they can wake up fresh, turn on the computer, make a cup of coffee and a delicious breakfast, and get right down to work. They can take breaks if they feel they need it without any colleague or supervisor possibly judging them. They're more relaxed when they get to work at their own pace. Their productivity levels increase throughout the day with the absence of stress and without the need to feel like they're in a rush all the time. The remote employee's job is not bound to where they live either. If their employer is alright with it and they've got the tools they need to get the job done, they could be anywhere in the world. On a beach in Bali, sitting outside by a sidewalk cafe enjoying the sunshine while they work, in their living room or home office, if that feels more comfortable. It's incredible what a refreshing change this could make both emotionally and physically when you take away the stress and the hassle of rushing back and forth to work and sitting in traffic.

## How Business and Work Environments Have Changed Since 2020

The Coronavirus or COVID-19 pandemic was a major catalyst for change in 2020 and brought a dramatic difference to the workforce that no one could have predicted. The biggest change of all being some businesses had to temporarily close their doors and order employees to work remotely to do their part and help curb the spread of the virus. Video conferencing and other technology to stay connected quickly surge in popularity and use during this period and businesses around the world almost simultaneously and without meaning to, followed in the footsteps of many Silicon Valley giants like Google and Apple. Business trips and conferences have been canceled, and never before in history have we seen something like this where businesses of every size had to forcible make remote working an option to cope and survive.

With the lives of billions depending on it, working from home in 2020 became a necessity for survival. From the United States to Europe, Asia to Australia, remote working was introduced as part of the solution for the required social distancing measures as one attempt to curb the rapid spread of the virus. However, telecommuting work like this can only exist if your job can be done on a computer or over the phone. Certain essential services like healthcare and food industries have had no choice but to remain open since the jobs require physical labor and could not be done remotely. Additional safety measures and precautions were introduced to keep employees as safe as possible, but any job that could be done remotely was enforced. What does this mean for businesses and the future of these businesses moving forward? How did this pandemic impact the way businesses operated and the measures they had to adapt to survive?

By far, the most obvious change was the way every business and organization had to quickly and with short notice, embrace a new remote way of getting work done. They have had to turn to technology to enable work to still proceed as planned and it has propelled the use of work-from-home software and solutions to the forefront. Businesses who were already embracing the remote working culture or already implementing it prior to the pandemic as an option for workers had a head start since they were already prepared with the tools they need. Other businesses had to quickly learn to adapt and find solutions to the challenges that came with not being prepared enough with remote working solutions. Expensive offices were now empty and eerily silent, devoid of any activity, and this raised the question of whether it was a necessity, after all, to be shelling out thousands of dollars in rent, expensive overhead costs, and utilities if jobs could be done remotely.

Service providers have become more crucial than ever in their role to help businesses and employees stay connected to avoid compromising on the quality of work. Internet traffic surged noticeably for both enterprise and consumer traffic. Existing remote working service providers also saw a spike in demand once employees were forced to work remotely. Both businesses and employees quickly had to adapt to the new way of working, and if there were businesses who thought remote working was not a viable option before, they've been proven wrong. It wasn't a smooth transition for many businesses though, especially the ones who were not prepared to deal with this sudden and drastic shift. Working remotely is not a challenge. It's been going on for a long time. It's not a new thing. Freelancers have been doing it for a long time, and they've found a way to make it work. The biggest challenge that today that employers are having with employees is the fact that employers don't necessarily trust that employees know how to deliver on their job, and the responsibilities they have because they've always been working out of an office. That's the biggest problem. All of a sudden pandemic happens, coronavirus happens, employees now have to work from home companies still have to pay you a salary and your bonuses. That's the problem the employer is struggling with, the worry of whether an employee is still going to deliver or take advantage of the fact that they're not in an office being scrutinized and monitored.

The work from home trend was given a significant boost in 2020 as remote working policies became mandatory by order of the government. The sudden switch to the digital way of work was a shift that happened almost overnight, and there is no doubt it has certainly changed the way businesses and employees started thinking about work from home arrangements. This proved to be a major tipping point for businesses to start giving some serious thought to the way things are being done. It also proved that a business can survive after all if an employee is not sitting behind a desk in an office. Work is still getting done, and in fact, some businesses are even seeing a boost in productivity among their employees. Will the coronavirus lead to a remote working revolution? The one thing we know for sure is that society is not going to go back to the way it was before. Not after everyone, both employers and employees alike, have had their eyes opened to the very real possibility, challenges, and benefits that come with remote work.

## How Businesses and Families Are Impacted by Remote Working

The truth is, all of its benefits, working remotely can have its struggles. Forming relationships and career development are significantly more challenging when you work from home. A Harvard Business Review study revealed that employees who worked remotely feel that their non-remote colleagues don't give them the fair and equal treatment that they should.

There are so many wonderful advantages to working remotely that it's a wonder why we didn't think about doing this seriously much sooner. Some of the perks of working from home include:

- **No Stressful Commute** - This is by far the most obvious advantage. It's very stressful battling traffic during rush hour, and by avoiding that completely, not only are you getting extra work time, but you're reducing your stress levels when you have to get to work and come home from work, and you're much better off because of that. That one hour or more you spend commuting to work in the morning can be spent getting in an extra hour of work done, making you a lot more productive than your commuting coworkers.

- **You Have Autonomy Over Your Work** - Unless you're in a role or specific hours are important, you can make your own schedule. Everyone can have a corner office because the world is your office. You can have their windows, you can have the food you want to eat, you can choose when there's music and when there's silence, and you get to decide just what temperature the room should be that is most comfortable for you. It teaches you discipline, and it teaches you independence. You and you alone are responsible for meeting the deadlines that have been assigned to you. Being accountable for your whether your work gets done or not will, no doubt, instill a greater sense of responsibility within you. You can choose to save the time that is spent commuting every day into getting more done a. A remote workforce is ideal for any company if they can find a way to make it work since responsible employees are what every business wants at the end of the day.

- **More Time for Family** - For working parents, remote working has been a dream come true for the many who want to spend more time at home with the children, so they don't miss a moment. Remote working has made it easier for both parents to work together as a team and juggle the responsibilities of running a household without having to compromise on the quality of their work. Sharing the responsibility and spending quality time with the family is one of the most priceless gifts made possible by working from home. For those who don't have a spouse or children to look after, the work-life balance afforded by remote work has made it possible for them to enjoy the quality of life more. They get to focus on work without compromising on the activities they love to do.

- **You Focus Better** - Let's face it, with the modern-day advent of open office spaces, they are a haven for distraction and interruption. While some people do enjoy the open concept of working and don't feel so restricted and confined in a cubicle, the downside of that is distractions, phone calls, and chatty coworkers are much harder to ignore. It's been drilled into us from the time we were in school about how important focus was if we wanted to succeed. To stay mentally alert and focused at all times when you're undertaking an important task. Focus, in a nutshell, is your ability to direct your attention towards one thing, and one thing alone. Focus is defined as deliberate action. You're deliberately concentrating on the one thing that you need to, and you're intentional about it, but this can be difficult to do when distractions threaten to break that concentration. The ability to work from home in the comfort of an environment you set up to be conducive for you is hugely beneficial to your ability to focused, productive, and efficient. Plus, you get to be completely comfortable when you're working when you know no one is watching or possibly judging the way you work (which can happen in an office setting).

- **Job Opportunities Around the World** - instead of having a job that you're looking for in your home city, a job that you're in right now, or even in their home country, imagine being able to find a job that you love around the entire world and being able to do it online. It opens the door for better prospects for you as an employee. There's a greater possibility that you'll find a job you're passionate about, and you love when you're not restricted by proximity anymore.

- **The World Is Your Office. Literally** - If you have the freedom to work from home, that doesn't actually mean you have to *work from home*. You have the choice to do that if you wanted, or you can work elsewhere like a coffee shop, or when you're on vacation and work remotely that way. You have the luxury of traveling to a new destination and spending 2 weeks, 3 weeks, maybe even a month there if you loved it without compromising your income because you still get your job done. The extra perks of being able to explore your new surroundings in between is a luxury that not many are lucky enough to experience. You can take your work with you wherever you go and have that location.

- **You Get to Live in Remote Locations** - Could you imagine being able to live anywhere in the world? You can even just work remotely for two weeks out of the year in a country that you want to live in or a city here and there. The opportunities to live anywhere are flexible, and the sky's the limit. It does depend on your relationship with your employer the time zones you're working for, but if you and your employer can come to an agreement, anything is possible.

- **Your Overall Health Improves** - With less stress comes a healthier and happier you. The health benefits you will experience and enjoy from having to work-life balance and not being locked into a very rigid and strict office schedule alone makes remote working worthwhile. You're going to be happier when you don't have to subject yourself to that stressful commute; you can avoid the flu season going into work, you can have more family time, you can enjoy more gym time. All that just by having that freedom of flexibility around your schedule that working from home affords you.

- **It's Environmentally Friendly** - With the greater environmental consciousness that has emerged and the necessity to reduce one's carbon footprint, working from how is how you can do your part. You're saving the environment by not contributing to the carbon footprint. From individuals to big corporations, it seems that everyone is concerned with going green these days to preserve our precious environment for the future. Working from home means relying on fewer resources, you are thereby reducing your carbon footprint impact and the amount of waste that you produce in the environment.

- **You Save A Lot More Money** - An employee living in New York, for example, could be spending over $100 a month on their MetroCard. Then there's also the cost of buying clothes specifically for the office environment that you're in or buying food every day or coffee or whatever you purchased during out the day where you worked. Food can be expensive, and it's that good for you since it's probably not healthy. Working from home, on the other hand, has a lot of cost-saving benefits to it. You're not going to spend money on gas, you're not going to spend money on parking, you're not going to spend money on unnecessarily eating out. Plus, you don't need as many clothes to wear because you don't need the professional attire that might be required for the company or the office space in a conventional job.

- **No Office Politics to Deal With** - Office gossip, worrying about whether you can fully trust your coworker not to steal all the credit for your idea, office politics are an additional and unnecessary part of working in an office setup that many people don't like dealing with. Working with so many different personalities means there is bound to be a clash of some sort. You're not going to get along with everybody, and not everyone is going to like you. All the unnecessary politicking can make it difficult to concentrate on work, and when you work remotely, you eliminate the need to deal with all that and focus entirely on your work.

- **You have the Flexibility of Running Errands** - Running errands during office hours would be almost impossible for those working in an office. To complete the errands they need, they would need to take leave, sacrificing on their precious off days just to get those errands done on time. Not a problem for someone who works remotely though. If you can juggle your time and work accordingly, running errands during the day is an achievable task as long as you can still meet your deadlines.

- **Fewer Sick Days Taken** - Employers will be the ones who benefit the most from this advantage. Where an employee might have otherwise called in sick and charged the bill to the company, remote working employees take fewer sick days since they can still get work done if the cough or cold does not bother them too much. With a better work-life balance and decreased stress levels, employees are less likely to fall sick as a whole when they don't leave their house much and potentially come into contact with sick people daily.

Of course, the grass is not always greener 100% of the time. Like everything else, there are challenges and certain disadvantages that come with remote work. For example:

- **When You're Out of Sight, You're Out of Mind** - A major challenge for employees who work remotely is to still feel like they are part of the team. These employees might feel like when they are not at work, they are not valued as much, and their work product is not valued as much. We've become so accustomed to the culture where you need to see someone in person to believe that they are working. When people don't see you sitting behind a desk, it's easy for them to make the assumption that you're not working. The company might not value you as much as an employee if they didn't see you every day.

- **The Constant Suspicion That You're Not Working** - Unfortunately, the old school style of working is a hard mindset to change for a lot of employers. If they don't see you at your desk, eight hours a day, they felt like you were not working at all, despite the fact that studies show most employees at work are only productive for actually four out of the eight hours that they're there. The rest of the time, they're either talking to other people, or they're doing things that are not that productive. An employee can still be at work and *not be productive,* and although many employers know this on some level, it's still a tough mindset to break out of.

- **There Are Distractions At Home Too -** Distractions are everywhere if you think about it. You've got distractions in the office and distractions at home. When you're at home, there are a lot of chores that need to be taken care of. You need to clean the house, do your laundry, walk the dog, pick up the kids from school, cook. The list is never-ending. Homelife can prove to have its own distractions. No matter where you go, there will be distractions, and it's a matter of how well you manage those distractions that make a difference.

- **Lower Pay -** Some employers believe that the perks of getting flexible hours mean an employee is going to be fine receiving a lower wage. But this also depends on the employee themselves. Some employees, especially the younger generation, would prefer more flexibility, work-life balance, and the opportunity to work remotely, and they're willing to take lower wages or it. Not all employees are happy taking a pay cut though, and this is something you do need to think about when you choose to work remotely. It's not always a case of being able to have your cake and eat it too, although, in an ideal world, it would be.

- **You're Not Going to Be Close to Your Colleagues** - Not unless you make an effort. You could be email friendly with them, but that's about it because it's not going to be the same as being there in person. Quickly turning to the person next to you to chat or ask a question, going to grab lunch together, chatting while you're making your cup of coffee in the break room. All the little things that build relationships are not going to be possible if you work remotely, and if you're a social person who loves interactions like these, working remotely can be a difficult adjustment.

- **There's No Such Thing As Fixed Office Hours** - The line between work time and personal time can become very blurry when your home doubles as your office. With the advent of computers, mobile phones, and the Internet, it has made it difficult for employees to disconnect from their work, as all smartphones are always at arm's length, staying connected all the time can lead to degrading health and increased stress. It helps to clearly define a time you need to commit to work. The hours can quickly tick by, and you end up spending long hours in front of your computer then you otherwise would have if you were at an office where you clock in and out. It can get messy and confusing unless you make an obvious effort to shut off your computer by a certain time and stop responding to emails. If you don't create very clear lines between work time and personal time, you might find yourself working insane hours and compromising on your family time when you do that.

- **Isolation** - Being alone most of the time can lead to feelings of isolation. When you barely leave your house since you can work right from your living room, the social interaction that you have are significantly reduced, and for some people, this can lead to feelings of loneliness and isolation.

- **Potential for Miscommunication** - Even working onsite miscommunication can happen from time to time. Working remotely, this can be even more difficult, and twice as difficult if you're working with teams from different countries. The challenges posed by cultural differences, miscommunication can be rife in virtual teams, but even more so when the team spans different cultures. A message that seems succinct to a team member in one country may come across as rude to a colleague from a different culture.

## Key Points Summary

Being on a virtual team and working remotely can present unique challenges that aren't faced by team members who are co-located, whether in another office location or at home. There are no managers or other teammates sitting nearby to consult with or provide immediate responses or support. Likewise, there's no one looking over your shoulder, keeping you focused and on task. Learning to manage the separation of work and home life is something that takes a bit of adjustment for both employees and employers. It's important to give yourself structure in the day and to have a proper diary so you can settle down work out what you're going to do today and work your way through it. Not everybody's that organized, but when you work from home, you need to be.

Employees need to learn to set boundaries, and employers need to learn to respect these boundaries and not take it for granted that an employee is always accessible just because they are working virtually. If there is no enforced nine to five schedules, it can be hard to maintain a proper balance. Often at home workers end up either working too few hours or conversely putting in an unhealthy amount of overtime. It's essential to put boundaries in place. The trick is to stay productive and minimize distractions, as well as limiting the potential for overwork and burnout.

For many, creating a designated work area is key to separating work and home life. Your workspace should have a clear physical boundary, and your work should stay within that space. It should be a work area that's not susceptible to disruptions. If you don't have access to a suitable area at home, choose an appropriate external site, but one where you can avoid distractions. Working in coffee shops, for example, may seem attractive, but a local library is probably a better choice. In either case, consider that working remotely nearly always requires an internet connection. Working virtually in a public place often mandates the requirement for VPN or similar secure connectivity. Another thing you need to do is get yourself a good workstation, make sure that you're comfortable where you're working that it's an easy, relaxed place and you've got all the bits and pieces you need to work Occasionally, get up and get away from your desk and walk around, perhaps settle yourself in another corner for a bit to do some work and then go back to your desk. Lots of fresh air if you can get it will help too. Go outside stretch your legs, all of those sorts of things are really important when you get around to working remotely.

People like to work in different ways and at different times and it's important to find out how you like to work when you're working from home because you're not in an office structure and you're therefore not being forced to work in other people's ways that you need to find your own. Some people thrive on work from home, and there are a lot fewer distractions, which is certainly helpful if you've got a role that requires a lot of concentration. But then again, then it can be very beneficial if you're the sort of person that gets their energy of other people to be immersed in an office situation. If you like the dynamics of in-person contact, then working from home can be a challenge. Some people love coming into the office; some people hate it. It will be tough for people who thrive in that office environment and that face to face interaction style of working side by side with their peers. Some people definitely have more of a preference to work at home for a variety of reasons that might be personal. It's really the individual difference but there are ways to make both situations work in a way that suits you best.

Whether working from home or a distant office, all virtual team members face the challenge of dealing with a lack of everyday face to face communication. and the team spirit that attends it working remotely. True, you do enjoy the benefits of spending more time with family, but for those who live alone or without a family, working remotely can potentially be a very isolating experience despite the benefits. Remote working teams miss out on the informal everyday interactions that co-located teams often take for granted. They miss out on nonverbal cues that indicate how their ideas and suggestions are being received. They can go days without contact, leading to feelings of isolation and virtual employees who feel isolated are less likely to contribute to the team. This will, in turn, erode both team spirit and team trust.

Businesses who manage remote working teams should recognize and capitalize on team diversity. Perhaps consider building a team profile, sharing each team member's experience, expertise, and personal information to minimize potential conflicts. Remote working teams should agree on ground rules for interactions that align everyone's expectations, like maximum response time to emails, agreed technology for sharing and updating files or guidelines on appropriate language and emails. But ultimately, regular daily communication helps counter these challenges. Cultivating a strong one-to-one relationship with your team leader, and if possible, other teammates help to mitigate these problems. It's good for morale and team unity if all team members regularly communicate about their progress, and where possible work together in partnerships. Even so, there is an isolation factor with working remotely that must be taken into account. It's important to make an effort to stay connected and informed, to make your presence recognized. A lack of closeness inhibits the formation of trust, connection, and mutual purpose, which happen to be the three necessary ingredients of a healthy team. It's important to be willing to take it on yourself to ensure that being out of sight doesn't lead to being left out.

# Chapter 2

# Remote Working Leadership

In 1979, IBM made headlines. It became one of the very first Fortune 500 companies to allow employees to work remotely. This proved to be so successful that by 2009, 40% of its 386,000 employees were enjoying the perks of remote working. However, in 2017, **IBM** decided to tell its thousands of remote workers to relocate to an IBM office or find a new job. Why did they do this? Because of the belief that bringing teams back to the office would make them more productive, innovative, and agile. Is working from home really less effective than working from a traditional office? Not according to a **Gallup report** that states remote workers log in longer hours, and are more productive than their non-remote peers. So, why is there still a debate about this topic? Well, mostly because it has a lot to do with the mindset. We've been so conditioned to believe that it is only when we're in the office under the watchful eye of many that we're "working productively."

## What It Takes to Be a Good Leader

Effective leadership can be nerve-wracking. Being an effective leader to a team of people who are counting on you to inspire them, to steer them in the right direction towards achieving a common goal is an even more overwhelming task. It's a lot of responsibility, and a leader is one that can effectively manage their team and bring out the best in everyone that is under their guidance. A successful leader is one that can bring out the best in everyone that they work with. They are the ones who know how to spearhead the journey to success. A great leader has a healthy mix of several qualities that contribute to their overall success. American author, speaker John C. Maxwell summed up the concept nicely when he said: *"A leader is someone who knows the way, goes the way and shows everyone else the way."* No matter which way you define it though, one thing you can be sure of is that a good leader can mean the difference between victory and failure. A leader needs to be a visionary, among many other things.

A good leader needs to possess the following qualities, especially when managing a remote working team:

- **Confidence and Belief in Themselves -** An effective leader needs to always display both confidence and assertiveness, a strength that others can take comfort in. You don't have to be overconfident, but you do need to reflect a certain degree of confidence, which allows your followers to develop trust in you as a leader. Before you can lead others, you need to be confident enough in your own ability to do so. Other people are not going to follow your leadership and commands if you are not sure about the decisions you make yourself. No one is going to believe in a leader who's always nervous and second-guessing their own decisions.

- **Integrity, Honesty, and Trustworthiness -** You must demonstrate the ability to stand by your core values and beliefs, and only when your followers see that they can place their trust in you will they become confident in your leadership abilities. Dwight D. Eisenhower, 34th President of the United States: *"Leadership's supreme quality is unquestionably integrity. Without it, real* *success is not possible"*. No matter which leadership position you hold, whether it's in a company, a sports team, an army, or any scenario in which you're in charge of a group of people, without integrity and honesty, you will never achieve true success.

- **Respect** - An effective leader constantly provides encouragement and helps their followers overcome challenges faced without belittling them. Respect is one of the major key principles that absolutely must be present. A leader must respect their subordinates to gain respect in return. Respect, however, needs to be earned, never demanded. When leaders don't respect their followers and vice versa, things can unravel really quickly, and not in a positive way. The best type of leaders and managers are ones that provide a work environment where employees help each other and value the contributions that everyone makes.

- **Inspirational, Passionate, and Committed** - As the leader, all eyes will always be on you, looking at how you handle the difficult situations. Being inspirational is probably one of the more difficult leadership tasks you could take on. You need to set a good example yourself if you want others to follow in your lead. As the 6th President of the United States, John Quincy Adams once said: *"You're a leader if your actions inspire others to learn more, dream more, become more and do more."* The ability to stay calm and composed under pressure, remain optimistic when others can't, to think positively and problem-solve creatively, that's what constitutes an effective leader. People are going to be looking to you to guide them, and they're not going to be motivated to do their best if their leader doesn't display the same passion and commitment towards achieving that goal. When a leader is not afraid to roll up their sleeves and get their hands dirty too, others will follow suit because of the commitment and the passion for getting the job done that is being demonstrated.

- **Maintain Consistency** - One of the worst things you could do as a leader is to appear disorganized and scattered. As a leader, you need to remember that everyone is looking to you for guidance, and it is you that they take their orders from. To be effective, you must be consistent in the way you do things. Be fair in your treatment and your rewards, be consistent in your methods of leadership, and be consistent in your principles.

## How Leadership Changes When Faced With Remote Employees

A lot changed in 2020 when companies globally had to resort to remote working to stay in business. Companies like Google, Apple, and any other big company you can think of, they've adopted remote work policies, all in an effort to keep their employees safe. Small to medium-sized businesses are following suit as well. They're taking a similar approach, getting their employees to no longer come into the office that they pay so much money for and to keep them safe by working from home. Here's the problem. Many leaders that are in positions of leadership have never led a remote team before, and leading a remote team can be very challenging. Notice the key phrase being used here is *leading,* not *managing* a remote team because those are very different things. A leader is someone whose actions inspire empower and serve in order to elevate others over an extended period of time. That's what leaders do, and if you're going inspire someone, breathe life into them, and you're going to empower them, you need to learn to let them make their own decisions. Yes, it is challenging because you don't get the day to day interaction that you normally would, in office.

How do we manage remote employees effectively? What steps should you take to build trust and open lines of communication when not everyone is on-site every day? How do you help remote workers feel part of the team when you're working with teams scattered across the country or the world? As the leader of a remote working team, you need to be a good listener, and not just listen for the sake of doing so either. You need to be able to listen actively and really pay attention to what your team has to say. You are the one they will go to when they feel something needs to be improved, and when your people feel that their leader is taking their every concern seriously, no matter how small it may be, and taking steps to fix it, they will feel appreciated and acknowledged, which will eventually spur them on to work better and perform better. Another quality you need to possess when managing a remote team is to have empathy. A leader can never make the meaningful connections they need to if empathy is not present. A leader that chooses to go with the dictatorial approach to leadership may get things done, but that doesn't necessarily make them a great leader. Being an effective leader means you need to be able to put yourself in your team's shoes, to understand their concerns, you're one step closer to making a difference in their lives and performance. That's how you become a great leader.

Remote working is very common these days. Finding remote employees and getting them on board is one part of the equation. Then comes the time to start managing them. So, let's look at ways you can do this effectively.

- **Create Ease and Friendliness** - When team members feel comfortable with each other, whether you are remote or not, the conversations, automatically become easier, direct, and friendly. Let's start with a few simple ways to do this in your online meetings. One thing that you can implement is to start your meetings with is to spend a few minutes talking about what's been happening in your lives, both professionally and personally. It doesn't have to be in every meeting, but at least a few of them. Truth is, you do this in person when you're working onsite, so why not virtually? Why is this important? Well, because sharing personal stories helps build empathy, which then paves the way for trust. You could even create meetings and call them virtual coffee or virtual hangout and make it very informal. You also don't have to be in every meeting, and you can encourage them to have their own meetings and talk about anything they want to.

- **Lead by Example** - You can't expect your remote workers to open up, get to know you, or discuss projects and share their opinion if you don't do that yourself. If you are in a leadership position, sharing your personal stories allows your team to feel comfortable sharing their personal stories as well. Likewise, be transparent with all aspects of the business, share with them the company vision and objectives. Let them resonate with that. Then set clear expectations and ask for input so they can share their ideas and opinions.

- **Establish A Chat Room That's Always Open** - Have a chat room open constantly. There are many platforms you can use. You can have chat rooms open for each team where everyone can share information or chat, just remember that while these are good to keep open communications, it's essential to keep these chats alive but not distracted. Share what you want, but don't necessarily expect an answer right away. Some employees might need to shut down such communication when they need to focus and don't want distractions. They will reach out at a later time, and that's okay. These chat rooms can have different subjects, business or non-business, and will create a similar watercooler ain to an office effect where you can hang out and build that team spirit.

- **Document Everything** - Document everything in an office so that it's easy to make decisions for all your employees, both who are in the office and working remotely. If people work remotely and some members of the team are having those conversations that the remote ones don't have access to, the remote employees will see these decisions being made without understanding why. Leaders need to now make it common practice for all employees to always leave a trail of where you were and what you were thinking about. This allows others to pick up where you left off. That's great for people in different time zones to interact and not feel like they've missed something important or feel left out in any way. It's also great to think about trying to have as much communication as possible online and documenting your conversations. When everything's shared, and all documents are made public, it allows new employees and those who work in different time zones to read through and catch up quickly.

- **Keep Your Work Organized** - Managing people across time zones without knowing what everyone is working on and having many projects on your hands can easily turn work into chaos. Therefore, you need to make sure you set goals and share them with everyone on the team. Share docs on a virtual drive, and encourage collaboration, then allow a degree of flexible work hours but also keep some consistency. People working from home will want flexibility with their work hours, and it's important to allow that. Trying to micromanage will be a nightmare. Instead, track their work and see what their output is. Are they delivering on time and as expected? Unless they have to interact with clients or team members on a strict schedule, it doesn't really matter if they work early mornings or late at night, as long as the work is done. Remember, they don't have a commute, so they might actually work put more hours in the day that you would put in the office.

- **Organize Frequent In-Person Visits -** Now, remote workers shouldn't be only always remote people, you need to make sure that you are going to visit them frequently, and on a predictable schedule. There are no rules about how often you need to see your remote workers in person, but it's important to do so, especially in the early stages. Invite them to your office during the onboarding period and continue visiting during the year. If your direct reports know there is an in-person visit every four months, it will help them build trust. Remember too, that remote team members often feel somehow invisible and that their actions and efforts are not noticed, so be generous with public praise and acknowledgment of remote employees.

- **Source the Right Tools** - There are so many apps and services that help with communication these days. Video conferencing, project management, you name it. Test out and experiment with different tools that enable collaboration, see what works. When it comes to conferencing, use screen sharing and video conferencing technologies, as much as possible. Sometimes just phone is great, but seeing each other is even better. If you are feeling uncomfortable with video still join, and you don't need to turn on your video every time. You'll have to do it sometimes, but it's not a forced thing if you're not comfortable with it, and it's important to let your employees know its okay for them to do the same.

- **Do A Big Meet-Up** - Organizations can come together for short, intense bursts twice or three times a year. Do a grand meetup where the entire company comes together for a week, for example, with the primary goal is connecting people. When you leave, you want to make sure that all your employees are aligned and on the same page. That they have a deeper connection with their colleagues.

- **Address Their Struggles** - If people have never worked from home, they're probably unaware of some of the hurdles or struggles that they're going to face when all of a sudden, working from their living room. Part of an effective leader's responsibility is to make people and team members aware of the typical struggles. Acknowledge their struggles and let them know you understand where they're coming from, and you're willing to work with them to find a way to resolve this.

- **Allow Flexibility** - Give employees the flexibility to make their own work environment. Every remote employee should ideally be provided with a remote working stipend they can put towards setting up a comfortable work environment in their home. This is money they can invest in getting the right chair, the right computer monitors, and the right desk set up so that they can have the most productive environment for them.

- **Cultivate A Sense of Security** - Your employees need to feel comfortable enough to be able to voice their opinions and concerns, even if they are not on-site to do it. If they are having difficulty working with another member of their team, they need to feel comfortable enough to approach you and bring up those concerns without worrying that there are going to be repercussions for themselves. It's important to give your remote workers a sense of security, especially when it comes to their job, so they're always reminded that they are still a valued member of the team. If an employee is constantly worrying about their job security and ability to raise their concerns, they'll find it difficult to concentrate on their job.

Just because the person is not there, it doesn't mean they're not working hard. In fact, employees who have the privilege to work remotely actually want to prove that they are working just as hard as their non-remote colleagues. They value the ability to work remotely more than you know, especially those who treasure the extra time they get to spend with their families and care for their kids. They value the opportunity to work from home so much that they're not going to do anything to jeopardize that, and employers should allow them the benefit of the doubt. That's what a good leader would do. You'll be able to see it in the work that they produce and let the finished product speak for itself.

You want to be extra attentive when you're managing a mixed-office team. When your entire team is remote, you will adjust more easily to work for a virtual environment. However, when half of your team is in office, and the other half remote, it can cause some problems. For example, your office team might decide to all the quick meeting and leave out the remote people who then end up not having their voice heard. So you need to make sure that all of your meetings are remote-friendly. This means that you are logged into whatever technology you are using and chat together through your computer, you must have everyone, the remote and local people all together and have the opportunity to share their thoughts and feelings.

## Micromanagement Is Not the Solution

A good leader trusts their team, whether onsite on remotely. A good leader measures performance based on the results of the work that is produced, not on how many hours your employee spends chained to their desk in a day. They trust their employees are responsible enough to get the job done, and they certainly don't resort to micromanagement because they know that is not the answer. The term micromanagement is defined as a person who is controlling and has to have their hands into everything, and they do not allow for others to handle anything without being scrutinized. You may *think* you are not a micromanager, but the chances are high that you are. At least sometimes, and when managing employees who work remotely, there's definitely a danger of venturing into micromanagement territory.

While it is a good thing that you want to ensure things are running as smoothly as they should, micromanaging is counterproductive. For all parties involved, but just the employee you're trying to oversee. If you tell employees exactly what they have to do and if you check everything you check their work down to the very last detail, then they lose the fun at work. The whole point of remote work was so that your employees could enjoy greater flexibility and work-life balance as part of the perks of the job, but when they are being micromanaged, they feel just as stifled at home as they would at work.

Here's where it gets tricky as a leader. It's okay to control results, and you need to do that because it is your responsibility to make sure work gets done so the business can keep running. But it's *not okay* to specify and control every tiny little step towards the results. If you don't give your employees at least some freedom to find their own way to get the result, then this is highly demotivating. Even worse, it might be so frustrating for them that they lose their desire to do any work at all, and their productivity levels drop, especially when they work remotely. Micromanaging makes it clear to your employees that you don't trust them and their abilities. Or at least, that's the message you're sending. There's another negative consequence that comes with micromanaging. Over time you train your employees to become dependent; after a while, you wonder why your employees don't seem to have any ideas of their own. This is not an ideal situation for both you and your employees to find yourself in, especially when more jobs are likely to be done remotely in the future.

Micromanaging managers often find it difficult to set priorities. Everything always seems important, and everything always seems urgent. Your employees are confronted with a flood of tasks that they need to get through. Sometimes, they need more time to work on a task and that's understandable when you juggle multiple things at a time. When managing remote employees, it's important to help them stay connected to the company, be part of the culture, and remember what the company's big picture goals and direction are. They cannot do that if their leader is too busy focusing on the nitty-gritty details of the day to day operations. When you micromanage, you're not guiding them towards the company's bigger picture. Micromanaging costs time and energy. Time and energy that could be spent in the leader doing something more productive instead of worrying about whether the remote employee is working as they should be. When you're a micromanager, you're the bottleneck of the company. If tasks are not completed on time, you're probably the reason why everything needs to happen through you.

## Changing the Style of Leadership

Let's get clear on some of the typical challenges that you're going to face right now as a leader who is in charge of a remote working team. Or if you're part of a remote working team, and you're not sure what you should expect from your leader. The first thing is there are real uncertainties and fear that come with working remotely when you've never done it before, and you're not sure what to expect. It's a natural thing because fear is the mental battle that goes on in all our minds. It's an emotional battle too and each of us experiences that battle in different ways. If you're going to go lead a team right now remotely, you have to understand your people are probably experiencing some real uncertainty and some real fear both about meeting the expectations of their job. Part of your responsibility in leading them remotely is to make sure everyone is clear on the fear that they're facing and how to overcome it.

The second big issue that comes with leading remote teams if you've never done it before is the technical issues. If you've never led a team via Zoom or only an email or only via Slack, technology can start to cause issues and not be of any help. You need to ensure that you and your team are equipped with the technology that you're going to use to best lead your team in a remote environment. The third challenge that comes with leading teams and a remote work environment like this is there's less work. Projects might not be the same; the workload might not be the same. Leaders need to be flexible enough to allow their teams to adapt. Everyone has to embrace flexibility. It's the only option to make remote working a success. Instead of treating your team like they have to be chained to their remote desk like they would have been in the office, now leaders have to say one of the benefits of leading working at home is that you have the flexibility to pick up your kids take them to school, go work out, go for a walk, eat dinner with your family. Your people will appreciate that. more than you know.

Working in an office is not a guarantee for productivity. For managers and co-workers to develop successful relationships with remote workers, there must be a change in the style of leadership. There must be some amount give and take and understanding from both parties. No one likes to feel like they're in the dark, and the best approach to managing teams that work remotely is to ensure constant communication is always a priority. Leaders should begin by setting expectations. Clear and honest communication is even more important for remote workers since these employees don't have the luxury of being able to swing by your desk to ask questions. For leaders to be effective, you need to schedule consistent catch-up sessions that are done other than through email. Pick up the phone or connect over a video call to make the conversation more natural.

Talent and intelligence are equally distributed throughout the world, but opportunity is not. In Silicon Valley, for example, you have the big tech companies fishing from essentially the same small pond. The talent that they acquire is then limited by the location they are fishing from. But remote working could change that. By making the company distributed, businesses can fish from the entire ocean, so to speak. Instead of hiring someone who grew up in Japan, but now lives in California as an example, companies can gain someone who lives, works, wakes up in the morning, and goes to sleep every night, wherever they are in the world. They bring a different understanding of a new culture and a different lived experience day to day, which, in a diverse world like the one we live in right now, is an advantage. As an employer, you can retain top talent if you open up your pool to the possibility of sourcing talent from around the whole world for that specific job you're looking for. It increases your chances of finding a candidate who is passionate about the job and the company that they work for, and as an employer, these are the kind of people you want on your team.

The other benefits of allowing your employees to work from home are:

- **Reduced Overhead Costs** - Employers can reduce the cost of the overhead of running an office and all the utility costs that come with having an office full of team members. After the coronavirus forced many companies to send their employees home and adopt a remote working approach, office spaces remained empty and silent, but the high overhead expenses were still putting a dent in the company's budget. Remote work eliminates the need for an office, and that could equal tremendous monthly savings for a business.

- **Working with Talent Around the World** - As long as your employee is getting the job done, it doesn't really matter where they live. As long as the work product happens, it doesn't really matter where they live, and you can count on them; you can trust them.

- **Adjustments in Salaries** - When working with remote teams, there is a possibility that employers could be paying less in terms of salary. That could be because of differences in the various economies if you're working with staff members from different countries. Or it could be that an employee is willing to work for less since they have the flexibility of working from their own home rather than have to spend money commuting to and from an office.

- **Talent Retention and Development Is Easier** - Recruiting and retaining talent is much easier when the employee has the freedom to work in a way that makes them the happiest. When you are one of the few companies who give the employee the option of working from home and value them, it makes them more likely to want to stay with your company. Flexibility is an attractive quality to many employees, especially with the modern mindset today that is starting to prioritize work-life balance and more quality time with family.

- **Increase In An Employee's Wellness -** A remote workforce could potentially equal fewer absences and sick leave for a business, which is also a cost-saving benefit. Research reveals that at least 75% of employees who worked remotely said they could still continue to work even if they had the flu. That same research also revealed that in the United States alone, absences that were unscheduled by the employees cost companies approximately $300 billion annually. That translates to about $1,800 for a single employee. With your employees working out of their own home and coming into contact less with people given that they no longer need to commute, the chances of them catching a cold or falling sick and passing it on to their coworkers are decreased. Fewer absences mean continuity in operations, and there's less likelihood that business operations are going to be heavily impacted.

- **Less Time Spent on Meetings** - With a remote workforce, the necessity for clear communication and distinct guidelines increases. With better communication all around, both the company and the employees will be clear on the goals and deliverables, and therefore, less time is spent on meetings. In fact, if all your employees are clear on what needs to be done, the need to hold frequent meetings is not as urgent anymore. When meetings are held via video conferencing, they are quick and get straight to the point so all parties involved can go back to working on the tasks they were supposed to.

# Chapter 3

# Analysis of Costs and Benefits

If you're like most people in 2020, you probably had to start working from home unless you were an essential service worker or in a type of job that could not be done remotely. If you were thinking about making the most to work remotely because you can't stand battling rush hour traffic anymore and you're looking for greater flexibility, no doubt you would have made a list of the pros and cons to support your decision. But have you considered the financial aspects of working from home? This applies to both employers and employees. Besides the salary, what are the day-to-day costs or smaller expenses you might be looking at if you decided to work remotely and give up the traditional office job life once and for all?

## Work From Home Statistics You Can't Ignore

Given the very real possibility that remote working is going to be a permanent part of the future job market moving forward, it's a good idea to know what to expect for both employers and employees alike. The numbers below certainly seem to be in favor of both parties and serve as proof that remote working definitely has a positive impact for both the business and the staff:

- U.S companies in 2018 saved an estimated $5 billion in costs with remote employees, and this was only with part-time workers. The savings factored in the diminished need for overhead, operating expenses, and real estate.

- PGI News reported that the average savings for an employer in terms of real-estate was an estimated $10, 000 per employee annually if they hired remote employees full-time.

- Global IT Recruiting company TECLA reported that work from home employees saved an average of $7,000 annually. The bulk of these savings came from not having to spend on food, clothing, commuting, and child care for those who had kids.

- OWLLabs reported in 2019 that remote working employees who worked from the comfort of their home at least once every month were 24% more likely to feel productive and happier at their work. Greater flexibility, better control over the way they worked, and their work environment, and not commuting to work played a big role in reducing the levels of stress they felt.

- An impressive increase in productivity among the staff who worked from home. A Stanford University study of 500 people who were both working traditionally and remotely revealed that productivity levels among remote employees are equivalent to a full day's work every week.

- There was 50% less attrition among remote workers, according to Stanford University researchers.

- Fudera reported that among the younger workforce, 68% of those surveyed said the ability to work remotely impacted their decision about whether to take up a job offer with a company or not.

- An Upwork report claims that by 2028, at least 73% of teams in businesses are going to have remote employees, especially with the demand being bolstered by the younger generation who are increasingly valuing work-life balance and flexibility. With the COVID-19 situation, it's likely that reality is going to be sooner than expected.

- The American Psychological Association reports that employees could easily reduce the amount of stress they felt if they had more control, and boost their motivation and growth as a result. Employees who enjoyed better work-life balance found more time to exercise, eat right, feel happier, and generally have a better outlook on life overall.

- Remote working is gaining traction, and in the last 10 years alone, it has grown by an incredible 91%, based on a FlexJobs and Global Workplace Analytics survey.

- Less need for Sick Day leave entitlements since remote employees are less likely to call in sick.

- Global talent pool means greater company diversity as the lines between culture, geographic location, race, ethnicity, and identity become blurred.

- Working remotely is reducing the gender gap in the fields of technology, according to one U.K study. Out of the women surveyed who worked in the tech field in the study, 76% said the option to work remotely was necessary to retain and attract females in this industry.

- Remote work increases the possibility for employees over 50 to continue in the workforce instead of being forced to go into retirement because they have no choice. This had a positive impact on the more senior staff, and companies could still benefit from their experience and by putting their skills to good use.

- It's a well-known fact that telecommuting means a decrease in greenhouse gas emissions, which is good news for the environment.

Remote working options are flourishing, and based on Buffer's 2019 State of Remote Work report; remote work is not going away anytime soon. In fact, it's here to stay for good as 99% out of the 2,500 remote working employees who were surveyed said they wanted the option to work from home some of the time for the remainder of their career years.

## Advantages and Disadvantages for the Company

When employees come to a physical office space to work, it is the company that foots the majority of the bill. They pay the rental, they pay the utilities, they provide the employees with the equipment needed to do work, they provide the office supplies, including snacks in the break room, and they pay for the internet needed to get the job done. That's part of the package. With remote working, there's no doubt that employers definitely save quite a bit in terms of not having to rent a physical office space and all the other associated costs that go along with it. But what about the expenses that are associated with remote working? Who pays for the employee's internet? Computer or laptop? What about the equipment needed, like a suitable desk and a comfortable chair to sit in for long hours? The employee is still getting the job done, but this time the office has moved into their homes. They're doing everything they would otherwise be doing in an office space, except they're doing it from home. So, is the employer expected to provide some funding to cover the necessary work-related expenses? And if so, do the employees need to take a pay cut? Those are a few of the questions that both parties should be thinking about before making the transition to full-time remote work.

Remote working is no longer considered an extra perk or benefit of the job reserved only for a select few who have earned the right to work from home after several years of service. Remote working is now the norm, and one study even shows proof that the number of teams who are quickly become fully virtual is on the rise. The year 2020, when organizations globally took to working remotely at the same time, was all the proof we needed to see that remote working is absolutely possible, and even better, it doesn't compromise on productivity either.

Stress has become such a common occurrence that a lot of us don't remember what it was like to live stress-free anymore. It is not uncommon these days for many to experience stress daily. Some people have found ways to regulate their stress and keep it under control, while others quickly unravel and go off the deep end as soon as they begin to feel the first signs of stress. Stress is a silent killer, and nowhere is this example perfectly illustrated than when we are overworked. Being overworked can take a tremendous toll on the body, mentally and physically. We may not feel it while we're working, but when it hits you, it hits hard. One day you wake up and realize you're dealing with a bad case of fatigued, completely exhausted, and burned out because you've been overworked for far too long. Stress, as we all know, is a contributing factor to a wide array of health concerns. The way society works these days; it's hard not to feel overwhelmed now and then. Juggling family life, social life, a career, your finances, planning for the future, it's almost too easy to get stressed these days. Stress is always going to be a part of life, so the way you learn to handle it is what truly matters. One way is by minimizing the stress that you feel while you're at work and with remote working, the greater degree of work-life balance is going to be of tremendous help.

By now, it's been established that the benefits of working from home include:

- Better work-life balance
- Time and money saved not having to commute to and from the office
- Ability to work anywhere you want
- Ability to work while you travel

But regardless of where and when you choose to work, certain things remain consistent. Like the need for the proper equipment to get the job done. Ordinarily in an office, all the necessary tools would be provided by the employer within the office itself, but what happens when the workforce is not remote? With remote work now on the rise, companies need to address the burning question of what are the cost benefits that stand to be gain that makes this type of work arrangement worthwhile for both parties. Remote employees can choose to carry out their tasks from one of three options. They either work at home, at a co-working space, or a coffee shop, library, and any other location they might find it easy to concentrate for a change of scenery. Some employees might even work while they travel to different countries and vacation simultaneously. These individuals are called digital nomads. Remote employees are still expected to work at the same time and maintain the same work hours as their on-site peers, but the reality is most of these employees enjoy flexible work hours as long as the job gets done and they attend the meetings they are supposed to. Every remote working employee is going to need three basic essentials when they work remotely:

- Proper furniture
- Equipment
- Necessary software and tools that all employees of the company need to use

So, to what extent is a company expect to foot the cost of the expenses? Does this same arrangement apply to freelancers since remote work and freelancing tend to overlap in certain areas? Ah yes, this very subtle difference needs to be addressed because *while most freelancers perform their duties remotely, NOT all remote employees are freelancers.* Remote working means you're employed *full-time* with one specific company as opposed to working per project the way freelancers do. Being independent, freelancers tend to foot their own bill, but this arrangement does not necessarily apply to a remote worker. Certain expenses are covered by the company for their employees who work remotely full-time, but it depends entirely on the industry and the company in question. Each company is going to have its own policy and way of doing things, so one remote worker's arrangement is not necessarily going to be the same as someone else. Here are some of the costs companies might be looking at when dealing with remote working employees:

- **Equipment and Furniture** - Companies should consider providing a one-off stipend for employees who are first setting up their remote working stations at home. However, the costs are only meant to cover one location, which is primarily the home. After all, the employee would be provided with a desktop, desk, chair, and printer if they had to work on-site, and they should have access to the same provisions when they are working remotely to as part of the job. Some companies might cover the cost of helping their workers get set up with a proper desk and chair and other work-related material they might need, but any additional extras would be at the employee's expense. For example, if an employee chooses to work in a coffee shop or while they're traveling, the employee would need to cover that cost. The company has already done its responsibility by providing the basic necessities.

- **Hardware and Software** - Like the basic office equipment, if the company requires an employee to have certain hardware or software to carry out their duties, then the company would need to cover the cost. The same way they would if the employees were working on-site. Remember, they're still working even though they're not sitting behind a desk in one location. If they are supplied with this equipment while they are in an office environment, they should be supplied with the same necessities even if they worked remotely. The software that is needed is going to depend on the job function and industry of the business. Designers, for example, require different software specifics compared to what a programmer might need. Those working in sales might require customer relationship management software and other types of marketing tools. All remote employees will likely require capable video and audio conferencing tools to touch base with the company and other members of the team. There is also a need for certain project management tools that would make work a lot more efficient. A company laptop would probably have all of these requirements already, but if the employee is using their own device, the company would have to foot the cost of installing and purchasing the software.

- **Internet** - This one is a bit of a grey area since most employees would already have established internet connectivity at home. One research found that out of the 1,900 remote working employees who were surveyed from 90 different countries, 78% of those surveyed were paying internet connection themselves. If your employee is already on a fixed internet package plan per month for unlimited usage and they've had no problems paying the bill thus far, then it's safe to say that they'll be more than happy to continue doing so as part of the perks of working from home. It should still be discussed with them to make sure they are okay with this. However, if the company does require that the employee upgrade their current internet package to meet the broadband speed demands needed for work, then the company should offer to cover the balance of the extra cost incurred.

- **Desktop or Laptop** - Most companies these days are happy to supply their staff with a company laptop for them to work on the go. Working remotely, this arrangement should still be doable. No extra expense is needed on the employee's part if they get to use the company laptop. If, however, the company requires a desktop, and the employee does not already have one at home, then this is something that needs to be discussed. Both parties need to establish if there is an actual need for a desktop, or if the job can be done using only the company laptop. Again, this would depend on the company involved, the nature of the job, and the company's policy when it comes to supporting remote employees. A company laptop might not be possible if the company is a small one with the budget to spare, and if that is the case, a discussion needs to be held with the employee to determine suitable work arrangements using the employee's current device.

- **Superannuation and Retirement Accounts** - This is the employer's responsibility, even for employees that work remotely. As long as the individual is employed with the company (not as a freelancer) and has a valid employment contract, they are still entitled to the same benefits as the on-site employees are.

How much the company is willing to provide financially is going to be entirely dependent on the company and what mutual arrangements they have worked out with the employees. There's no hard and fast rule, but if a company and the employee can come to an arrangement that everyone is happy with, the positive ripple effect from this is going to be evident in the quality of the work produced. The cost of helping the employee set themselves up with everything they need to work efficiently from home would still be much cheaper overall than having to pay for rent and the overhead costs that come with running an on-site office. Especially when rental prices spike in major cities. **PGi reports** that full-time work from home employees can result in a company saving as much as $10,000 annually per employee in terms of real estate savings. Health insurance giants like Aetna, for example, managed to do away with 2.7 million square feet without the need for an office, which in turn resulted in the company saving **$78 million annually.** You certainly don't need an office these days to run a full-fledged business, and remote working teams can equal significant savings for the business overall.

There is also the issue of workplace health and safety and insurance. While employees are unlikely to experience any work-related accidents if they don't' leave their home to commute to work, there are still some unique health and safety considers that an employer needs to consider. Physically, an employee that is not set up with the proper ergonomics to work behind a desk long-term is likely to experience some posture and physical related issues while on the job. Medical benefits and basic insurance coverage should continue to remain part of the employment package offered, even for remote workers. Remember that they may not be on-site, but they are still working on matters for the benefit of the company, no matter where they may be. Not being on-site does not make an employee less valuable, and if they are employed full time, they should still be provided with basic health and insurance coverage, the same way on-site workers are, even if they end up not using it in the end.

## Advantages and Disadvantages for the Employees

Offices are not always the ideal type of work environment for everyone. Of course, since people are different, some are going to prefer the dynamics of working in that kind of setting, while others may prefer a more remote option. In early 2020, many employees found themselves working from home not by choice, but out of necessity since businesses were ordered to close temporarily as part of the enforced social distancing measures to curb the spread of the COVID-19. Some employees were no doubt thrilled by the idea. The daily commute quickly became non-existent, they had a lot more control over the kind of work environment they wanted to set up for themselves, and probably the best part was there was no need to change into your office wear. You could be working in your pajamas all day if you found that more comfortable. Probably the biggest challenge was not having any bosses or colleagues around, which made it difficult to stay on top of the tasks they had to do. Being accountable for all their decisions and actions now that they were working independently was no doubt a bit of an overwhelming experience for some employees.

What a lot of employees working remotely for the first time might be underprepared for is the costs involved with setting up your workspace. If you have never worked remotely before until now, it's unlikely you would already have an in-home office setup or designated area declared as your workstation. There's no hard and fast rule as to how your home office should be set up, but you definitely want to get yourself organized with a designated work area to help you stay focused. Once in a while, if you want to move to the couch or dining room for a change of scenery, by all means, go ahead and do it. But ideally, a home office is still a necessity, and there are two main factors you need to consider when setting up this area solely for work:

- **Separation** - Remember how some employees find it hard to separate work and personal life when they work remotely? Well, this is why you need a separate area for one specific purpose. In this case, your home office should be a separate area that is solely for work and nothing else. The rest of your home can be well used for rest and relaxation and any other activities you want to get done, but in your home office area, it's all about work. The environment that you surround yourself in has a certain level of influence on our psychological state of mind. When you're stressed out by your environment, it makes it difficult to concentrate on anything, and you know this from your days of working in an office. Being distracted and unable to focus on anything else except your stress is how you slowly start to burn out and feel demotivated over time. Your external physical environment can contribute to the way that you feel, and if you need more proof, just think about all those times when you were stressed out in a chaotic office environment. You want to give your brain it's best chance to stay on task by not being too distracted by your external environment.

- **Isolation** - If you don't live alone, you need to be isolated to minimize your chances of being interrupted when you need to stay on task. Or even when you need to host a virtual meeting with your boss and the rest of your team. It simply won't do to have pets, kids, partners, or spouses running around in the background or creating a lot of noise when you're trying to stay focused on your meeting. The rest of your team is bound to be distracted by what's going on in *your* environment too, and the meeting is going to end up being nothing more than a waste of everyone's time. Not being isolated enough is a big problem in many office setups too. Chatty colleagues, colleagues on the phone, and various other noises can interrupt your train of thought all too easily. It becomes an even bigger issue when you're at home with family and this is something you have to take into consideration once you decide to go down the remote working path. Which is again why you need a designated space or room for your home office.

Now, you already know that you're going to be saving money commuting, buying a cup of coffee and bagel from Starbucks every morning, eating out for lunch, and on the clothes you have to wear, but what about the costs *incurred* by working from home?

- **Your Utility Bills** - Now that you're working from home, your utility bills are going to be much higher when you're not spending 8 hours away outside and at the office. Prepare to see a spike in your utility bills when you make the transition to work from home and factor that into account when you're working out the salary negotiations with your employer.

- **Your Taxes** - If you're employed by a company, then you probably don't have to worry about this aspect since the employer will take care of it for you. If you're working independently as a freelancer or an entrepreneur in charge of your own business, then a chunk of your earnings still needs to go towards taxes even if you're self-employed. You'll want to discuss this with your accountant before making the leap, so you know exactly the kind of costs you will be looking at tax-wise.

- **Health Care Costs** - If you're employed by a company, then like your taxes, this is something you don't have to worry about too much either. But if you're working independently, then you're going to have to bear the cost of your own medical expenses. This additional expense is something to take into account since it will have an impact on your take-home salary.

- **Health and Insurance Coverage** - Yes, working remotely may result in better health without the need to commute and being able to pace yourself when you work, but health and insurance coverage is still something you should not skimp on. Even if the company does not provide basic insurance benefits, this is something that you should establish independently on your own to protect yourself. If the company you work for does not offer insurance, consider the costs of the monthly premium and see if the cost can be worked in when you're negotiating a salary package.

- **Home Office Setup and Equipment** - If you haven't already got a designation work station for yourself, then you'll need to set yourself up with one if you're planning to give up traditional office life in favor of working remotely. The cost of setting up your home office is going to differ based on what you've already got that you can use and the things you don't have yet that you need to buy. It's going to be different for everyone. You're going to need to invest in a proper desktop or laptop (depending on whether you need one or both), a printer, and a scanner, perhaps even a copier if you need it. You're also going to have to invest in high-speed internet so you can conduct your meetings with the rest of your team virtually (unless you're working independently).

- **The Cost of Groceries** - You'll be spending less money buying take out food, but your weekly grocery bill is bound to see a spike when you're spending more time at home. More home time means more meals needed at home now that breakfast and lunch are no longer going to be external affairs.

## Do the Benefits Make It Worthwhile?

There is no denying that remote working has some major cost-saving benefits for both the business and the employee. However, at the end of the day, it is up to the employee to determine if the perks and the financial savings are going to be worth the realities that come with working from home. Not everyone operates the same way, and some people crave and thrive on the social interactions they get daily from meeting their colleagues and being physically present to work together in a team. Even the flexibility and better work-life balance might not be enough of a benefit to compensate for the loneliness and isolation that is often felt with remote work, especially if you live alone and don't have a family just yet.

For the employee, it is important to give some serious thought to before making the transition. It is up to you to decide if remote working is going to be a good fit for your personal and financial goals, especially where the salary package is concerned. Having a tight budget every month can quickly take the fun out of being able to work in your living room in your pajamas all day. Besides the work-life balance, cost-saving in certain aspects, and the flexibility of setting your own hours and style of work, there's another big reason why one might consider remote work full time. *To reduce the daily stress that you feel.* Being excessively stressed every day is one of the major reasons why so many people feel overwhelmed. Even when, in reality, their circumstances are manageable, the worry that they experience is affecting their ability to see clearly.

Everything feels like a big deal when you're overwhelmed. Everyday stress could be triggered by information overload, a routine that is too hectic, pressures at work, and even if you happen to be dealing with several mental health issues like anxiety, depression, or panic attacks. Excessive worry and stress is a debilitating condition to deal with. It is a taxing emotion to go through for a long period, and it will take its toll on both your mind and your body if nothing is done to keep it under control. It starts with stress before it eventually leads to other mental health conditions, depression, and anxiety among them. Stress can cause severe disruption in your ability to focus. When you're stressed, the simplest thing or task can appear to be something overwhelming. Your behavior might become frantic and erratic, even unpredictable as the stress piles on until you finally reach a point where you can't think clearly anymore. Being in a state of frequent emotional turmoil can lead to stress, which, as we all know, is never good for the body. The elevated cortisol levels, adrenaline pumping through our veins, they are referred to as "stress hormones," and when they course through our bodies, they're pumping us up to react in a way that is quick and strong. Unfortunately, it is also difficult to concentrate when you're in this state.

For all these reasons and more, remote working is quickly becoming a more appealing option, especially to the younger generation. Better quality of life eventually leads to elevated levels of happiness, and there's no reason why you have to sacrifice one for the other when we live in a world of options these days. The happier you are, the more it shows, even in the simple day to day tasks that you have to manage on the job.

# Chapter 4

# Organizational Survival Kit

A successful leader and manager is one that can bring out the best in everyone that they work with. A good leader is one that knows how to spearhead the journey to success. As the leader of a remote workforce, there are a few rules of thumb to think about when you're trying to communicate with a remote workforce:

- **Stick to the Agreed Upon Norms** - This can help to eliminate a lot of confusion and miscommunication. It is always easier to deliver a message when it is done in person. It minimizes the chances of miscommunication happening, and it allows you to get a better read on the situation you're being faced with, and where remote working is concerned, important messages should ideally be delivered in real-time via video call. That's one example of an agreed-upon norm that could be implemented. It could also be in the form of agreed response times or standardizing the use of platforms that are used across the company. The important thing is for all team members and key players involved to be on the same page to make collaboration as effective as it can be.

- **Defining Your Goals** - A good leader is one who is clear on what the organization's goals are and what needs to be achieved, and they would need to communicate these goals with the rest of their team, so everyone is working towards the same thing. You need to rally your remote workforce around goals that have been clearly defined and a good leader needs to take ownership of that. Devise a plan to turn those goals a reality together with your team and this effort helps to ensure that everyone feels included.

- **Avoid Brevity Where Possible** - Unless you and your team already have an established list of shorthand protocols that are always in use, it is best to avoid making the assumption that other people in the team are going to understand your brevity. Invest in a little extra time to make the message extra clear to your team. It's always better to have the message delivered loud and clear rather than risk misunderstanding along the way, which could jeopardize the quality of the work that gets produced.

- **Don't Overdo the Communication** - Bombarding your team with one email after another, several phone calls, and multiple text messages are only going to overwhelm them. Imagine that each email you send out is as if you were walking physically to your colleague's workspace and piling the requests on them. It's overwhelming, and as anxious as you may be to make sure the job is done, you need to pace yourself and be flexible with your expectations. Give your team members a reasonable response time, given that they are working remotely. This is where an agreed-upon set of norms would come in useful. Keep your digital volume down to a minimum and think carefully before hitting the "send" button.

- **Be Consistent In Your Guidance** - There is nothing worse than a leader who is scattered all over the place. As a leader, you need to remember that everyone is looking to you for guidance, even if they are remote. It is you that they take their orders from. In order to be effective, you must be consistent in the way you do things. Be fair in your treatment and your rewards, be consistent in your methods of leadership, and be consistent in your principles.

- **Make All Ideas Feel Like They Matter** - There are going to be some people in your team that have better ideas than the next person, it happens. But as a leader, if you want to be successful and effective, it is your job to listen to everyone's ideas, even if they are not necessarily good ones. Make it your personal policy to encourage anyone with an idea to approach you and give them a chance to express their ideas. Your job is to be encouraging, regardless of whether the idea gets used or not.

- **Transparency Is Necessary** - Your remote team is not going to see you every day, and they need to feel secure enough in your leadership to trust you. Being open, honest, and transparent in everything you do as a leader will show your team that you lead with integrity and honesty, and this will help to strengthen their trust in you. Trust and respect go a long way in successful and effective management, and if your team doesn't respect you or trust you as a leader, your team will be doomed right from the start with no hope of success.

- **Be Accommodating To The Introverts** - The more introverted members of the team will really enjoy the aspect of remote working that lets them work at their own pace and within a comfort zone that is easy for them to concentrate in. It is important to keep the introverted members of the team in mind and be attentive to their needs, so they continue to feel nurtured and valued by your leadership, even when they're working remotely. Perhaps they benefit and prefer written forms of communication rather than constant video calls every other day.

- **Be Respectful Toward All Team Members** - Respect is one of the major key principles that absolutely must be present with a team and an organization and even more so among a remote workforce. Respect among leaders and the people that they lead is the glue that keeps the team successful, and when there is no respect, things can unravel really quickly, and not in a positive way. The best type of leaders are ones that provide a working system where employees help each other and value the contributions that each individual makes. Effective leaders constantly encourage their peers to bring their A-game to work every day and help them overcome the challenges faced without belittling them. In a remote workforce, respect will be the key to keeping your team strong, united, and happy.

- **Socialize and Celebrate** - Find little ways to celebrate and socialize with your team to help strengthen relationships, even though you may not be seeing each other in person every day. Even a simple gesture like group video calls to wish a member of the team happy birthday can be a way of boosting rapport and a sense of belonging among the group. All work and no play makes for a very dull and demotivated team. Every now and then, you need to break the monotony, let loose and have a little fun to recharge your team, especially if they have been working hard towards meeting a goal or a deadline.

- **Organize In-Person Catch Ups** - Go out for lunch together, organize a team get together outside of work for a fun activity, when someone in the team is having a birthday, make a celebration of it. Or maybe even for the heck of it, just go for a movie together as a team. There are lots of ways that a leader can bring a little fun into the mix.

- **Make Connections** - Connecting and engaging with team members shouldn't only happen when an online meeting takes place. Go the extra mile and make a connection with each member of your team. Build a connection that is meaningful that shows your team members you genuinely care about them and their welfare, not just because it is part of your job to do so. Set an example by reaching out to them on a regular basis, congratulate them on little victories accomplished, remember special moments like their birthdays and anniversaries. These efforts will go a long way in keeping your team happy.

The challenges of managing a remote working team are not going to disappear entirely, but having a set of consistent rules, protocols, and an organized way of conduct will go a long way.

## Managing Your Remote Team Effectively

It's not easy being in a position of leadership. The dynamics of the work environment and setup are constantly changing. Years ago, no one could have predicted we would one day be able to work right from our living room without ever leaving the house. No one might have anticipated we would one day see leaders managing teams virtually. Being a leader is not easy. Not only are you responsible for your own work, but you are also responsible for inspiring, leading, and motivating a team of individuals under you to be the very best that they can be every day at work to achieve the set goals. The toughest thing about guiding and managing a team of people remotely is working with all the different personalities and getting those personalities to work together effectively and successfully. No two people are the same in a team, and there is no one-size-fits-all approach that can be taken because of how different the people in a team can be.

Leadership takes persistence and perseverance, and most of all, a lot of patience on the part of the leader. Leaders need to constantly evaluate their leadership method to see if their approaches are working as well as they should. When everyone in a team can successfully work well together and is the embodiment of what the word "teamwork" means, then you will know you are on the right track. They also need to know the strengths and weaknesses of each member of the team, remote employees included. A good leader is one that delegates the right jobs to the right people, so they come away with excellent results because they know just what to do when a job is given to them. People have been known to become better performers and become more engaged staff when they feel they are really excelling at the tasks at hand, and you would be surprised at just how much this can impact the productivity in a team.

One of the biggest challenges as the leader of a remote team is keeping that team spirit alive. Now, more than ever is when you need to be a walking embodiment of the phrase: *There is no "I" in a team*. Meaning, that any success in a team is achieved as a team, with everyone pulling their weight equally, and it's important that both on-site and remote employees are included in this.

The best way to spur your team to keep on performing to the best of their abilities? By openly acknowledging when a job has been well done. A good leader is one who not only congratulates the team for a job well done but also provides the right kind of feedback on what can be improved on to do even better. There's a lot of tact involved here because you don't want to end up saying the wrong things and making your team feel that all their efforts are not appreciated just because there are some areas that can be improved upon. Constantly encourage your team and always acknowledge when a job has been done well to give them the drive to keep going.

## How to Prepare and Track Online Meetings

Online meetings are now an increasingly popular way to connect work when you can't physically be at the office. Traditionally, meetings can sometimes be one of the biggest waste of time in office culture. You might even say that five out of the 10 meetings that you sit in are either unnecessary or, at the very least inefficiently run. In a remote work setting, the likelihood that meetings are going to continue to be a time-waster is increased even more, especially if you don't figure out beforehand what you're going to talk about or whether the meaning is even necessary in the first place. Some things, by their very nature, are just not a good use of group time. For example, if you're trying to get feedback on an extensive document, something like that might be better handled offline. On the other hand, if items are sensitive or require significant back and forth or clarification. They can be a great use of meeting time.

Meetings are resource-intensive, and they take up people's time. Most people mistakenly think that if you schedule a one-hour meeting on the calendar and if the meeting is not productive, then you've only lost one hour of time. But in fact, you have to look at it in terms of the number of people-hours exhausted. If you have five people in your meeting, and you've had a one-hour meeting that's not one hour of wasted time. That's *five hours of wasted time*, one for each person, and from there, it's pretty easy to quantify how much a meeting is costing either your company or your clients depending on how your business is set up. Just multiply those hours by the salaries of the employees involved or your billable rate. One fair way to do it is to assign delegates from each department so that you have one person representing each group or department. Their job is to represent that team, and then filter that information back to them and make sure that their interests are represented and so on. The same principles can apply to virtual team meetings too, where the leader holds an online conference with the respective heads of department, who might then pass the message along to the rest of the remote team members.

Tracking your online meetings these days is easy, with the multiple video conferencing options available. You can see exactly who is logged in to your meetings, and holding group conferences has never been easier. It's preparing for the meetings that require a little extra work. Here are a few tips to follow as you make preparations to participate in your online meeting:

- **Test Your Tech** - It's always a good idea to set up and test your tech and equipment *before* the meeting starts, so you're not wasting any time fumbling at the start of the meeting trying to get your microphone or your camera to work. Make sure these are all in working order well before your meeting, not during. Joining the meeting early is recommended if you can, especially if you're going to speak during the meeting for just this reason.

- **Getting Rid of Background Noise -** Conduct your online meetings while sitting in a quiet space and try and eliminate any noises that may be distracting, including putting your phone on silent. Your microphone may pick up background noise, and that can be a major distraction for other meeting participants. Mute your microphone whenever you aren't speaking. This simple step is an easy way to guarantee that background noises, movements, breathing, or other sounds are not going to be a source of distraction. Don't distract from whoever is currently speaking and when it's your turn to speak, remember to unmute your microphone.

- **Invest in A Good Microphone -** Video conferencing tools like Zoom will automatically check for available output devices and allow you to change your preferred audio output source, such as laptops speakers, desk speakers, or headphones. However, if you're not using Zoom, it's a good idea to invest in a proper set of headphones if you don't already have it. While most laptops and computers today do have built-in microphones, they're often not the best quality or the loudest, so it might benefit you to look into purchasing a simple USB mic or headset to improve your sound quality. You can even use simple headphones with an inline mic like the ones that you might get with an iPhone. Proper meeting etiquette suggests wearing your headphones to keep your speakers from echoing back into the audio feed.

- **Maintaining Good Eye Contact** - Eye contact is an important part of any speech, and it's something that people struggle with when meeting online. The best way to mimic eye contact online is to focus on your webcam and not your screen, or anything else around you. Place your webcam app around eye level for the most flattering angle, and to keep the wide-angle lens of the camera from distorting your face. Even if you're feeling shy, it's important to find a way to cope. If everyone else has their webcams on, it's proper meeting etiquette for you to do the same.

- **Consider Your Background** - If there's anything in your background that may be distracting, try and move it before the meeting. Some online meeting platforms allow you to blur your background, while others allow you to change it altogether. These are both good options to hide what otherwise might distract speakers and fellow meeting participants.

- **Using Proper Lighting** - If you're going to be on camera during an online meeting, you need to have proper lighting. It's important to make sure others can see you. To ensure that happens, work in a well-lit room and avoid having any lights point directly at your camera. Traditional webcams work by automatically adjusting your settings based on the brightest part of the image. So, in order to get the best out of your webcam video, you want the brightest part of the image to your face. Move away from bright objects behind you, such as lamps and windows to prevent your image from blowing out or becoming too bright in the wrong areas, leaving yourself in the dark. Instead, you can place yourself in front of these objects to light yourself. Keep in mind that if you move too close, you'll start looking a bit pale and if you move too far away, you'll start fading into the darkness of the background. The best practice is to evenly like both sides of your face using either too small or one large source of light near us such as table lamps or ring lights positioned at or slightly above eye level to prevent casting unflattering shadows.

- **Be Natural** - Treat it like any other meeting. Online meetings may be awkward at times, but behaving as you normally would, in person will make it less so. If you wouldn't do it during an in-person meeting, don't do it in an online one. Dress, speak, and behave as you would during any other meeting, and you'll be just fine. It's also important to remember that once you join a meeting, there's always a possibility that your webcam is on and that someone is able to see you. Dress appropriately, at least from the waist up. If you don't stand up, you can be wearing anything for pants, and no one would be none the wiser.

- **Avoid Being Distracted** - Remember that just like in a face to face conversation, it's all too obvious in online meetings when you're too distracted or if you're looking off to do something else. Be engaged by keeping yourself in the camera view and looking at other people that are talking in the virtual meeting.

- **Username and Profile Picture** - Encourage all members of the team to use their real names and profile pictures to make it easy to identify the participants in the chat room before the meeting commences. Putting a name to a face will make it much easier for everyone involved to know exactly who they are speaking to, especially for the new staff who join the business.

- **Time Zone Confirmations** - If you're conducting virtual meetings with employees based in different time zones and locations around the world, confirm the time zones beforehand so everyone is on the same page about what time the meeting should start. Time zones can be a tricky one to navigate, so be sure to confirm well in advance a suitable time that works for everyone who is going to be involved in the meeting.

- **Be on Time** - Make an effort to be punctual, especially if you are the one who is hosting the meeting. Time is money, and you don't want to be wasting anyone's time *or* wasting time waiting for members of the team to join before the meeting can commence. You wouldn't be late for an on-site office meeting, and it is important to remind your team to maintain the same punctuality etiquette as this is still a professional meeting that is being conducted.

- **Call If There Are Last Minute Changes** - If you or any member of the team has a last-minute conflict or emergency that prevents you from attending the meeting, it is best to pick up the phone and give the people who are going to be involved in a meeting a heads-up. Since it is at the last minute, they might not check their emails in time, so a phone call would be more appropriate in this instance.

- **Dressing Presentably** - You might enjoy the luxury of being able to work in your pajamas, but if you know there is going to be a business meeting video call scheduled, proper etiquette requires that you dress appropriately for the meeting. It simply won't do for the rest of the virtual team to see you rumpled or disheveled like you just rolled out of bed (even if you did). Be presentable and dress the way you would if you were attending an on-site meeting. Professionalism is still necessary, even when working remotely so your team members can take you seriously.

- **A Quick Round of Introductions** - Where necessary, always do a quick round of introductions and acknowledge everyone who is on live during the virtual meeting. New employees will appreciate this and feel welcomed. If you are aware that not everyone in the meeting might be familiar with each other, do a quick round of introductions and mention the names and various departments that are currently participating in the meeting.

- **Internet Connection -** Even after all this prep, the meeting can still fall apart if you have a poor internet connection. Always check your connection before you begin your meeting. If you're on a laptop, move closer to your Wi-Fi router and close down all unnecessary applications on your computer that rely on an internet connection. If you're on a cell phone or a tablet, try switching your connection to Wi-Fi instead of cellular data because data plans can often cap your internet speed to very low numbers, which will result in choppy audio and drop meeting calls. You can always check your internet connection speed by going over to Google and sourcing for an internet speed test website like SpeedTest.net. A good standard speed is about 20 megabits per second for download and five megabits per second for upload. That's a loose guideline to use as a point of reference, and it really depends on your internet provider speeds.

## What to Do After the Meeting

Once the meeting is over, as the leader, you're going to be responsible for following with the rest of the team to make sure everyone has a clear idea of what their objectives, next action steps, and deliverables are. Once the minutes of the meeting have been finalized, send an email to all the meeting attendees. The attendees should be clear on the following aspects:

- What are their next action steps moving forward
- What they are responsible for and what needs to be reported at the next meeting
- What are the expected deliverables and deadlines
- Who is the person in charge of each deliverable that has been set
- The time and date of the next meeting to check-in and report on progress

Touch base with each meeting attendee individually too and have a quick chat about how well they thought the meeting went. A quick phone call will suffice for this one, and all you need to do is confirm they're happy with how the meeting went and if they would like to clarify any questions or concerns that they might have felt too awkward to raise in front of the rest of the team. Alternatively, you could create an anonymous feedback survey if your team members are more comfortable with that approach. Feedback is always appreciated for ongoing improvement to make virtual meetings even better moving forward.

Seeking feedback is part of making yourself an accessible leader, even more so when you're managing a remote team. Making yourself accessible here means making yourself not just an approachable figure to your team who is willing and ready to listen to their complaints, but to be a successful leader, you need to make yourself open and accessible to receiving criticism too. No one likes being criticized, and it takes real courage for a leader to make themselves open to it because no one ever likes listening to negative things about themselves. But avoiding the issue is not the way to go, and if your team feel like you are willing to give and receive, and listen to criticisms with an open mind, in the long run, it will benefit everyone (both leader and the team) because when you know what the weaknesses are, you can work to improve on it. And that is what being successful is all about.

If you have questions for your team, don't be afraid to speak up and ask either. Just because you are the leader, it doesn't necessarily mean you have all the answers to everything. The worst thing you can do as a leader is to pretend that you know it all and to end up making a mistake in the end because of poor judgment. A successful leader that practices transparency will be honest if they do not know for certain what the answer may be. A successful leader doesn't pretend to know it all for the sake of keeping up appearances but instead tries to gain access to the resources that are able to provide those answers and then share them with the team.

## Best Tools to Backup and Secure Documents

Keeping your files safe and secure is not a problem anymore with the myriad of tools available. Saving documents and backing up your files is the greener way to go, in fact. You save the environment by not using as much paper, and you keep your files safe in the cloud, and there they will remain forever until they get deleted. Many of these options are available for free too, so there is no reason not to backup your work. It cannot be emphasized enough just how important it is to always back up your work. Imagine spending hours on a document only to lose it or accidentally delete it? That's hours of hard work that you've put in gone in a matter of seconds. There always needs to be copies of important company documentation online other than your computer hard drive, since a hard drive crash could also happen when you least expect it.

Store your documents on a USB drive, a hard drive, an external hard drive, *and* store them in the cloud too. Cloud backup tools like Google Drive and Dropbox have made it much easier, and it's a good idea to have multiple backups on separate devices. That way, if one gets compromised, you still don't break a sweat when you know you've got a spare. Access your files anytime and anywhere while you're on the go on any device with any of the following options to choose from:

- Google Drive
- Paragon Backup and Recovery
- Dropbox
- Cobian Backup
- Microsoft One Drive
- Office 365
- Nakivo Backup

Remote working teams can easily collaborate on the same document and make changes in real-time with the right tools. Who says working in a team has to be difficult when you're working remotely? File-sharing tools eliminate the need for multiple documents and multiple files when several people can work on one document at once. Most cloud services and file-sharing services come with extensive security measures, making this the much safer option in the long run. One document, multiple people, and one perfect finished product later are absolutely possible with some of these excellent file-sharing options:

- Google's G Suite on Google Drive
- Dropbox Business
- Microsoft's One Drive for Business
- Apple iCloud (although this option is limited to only Apple and iOS devices)
- File Whopper
- Box Business
- File Cloud
- Citrix File Share

# Chapter 5

# Remote Working Survival Tips

For many employees, having the flexibility of being able to work from home has been a dream they've pursued for a long time. There are indeed real benefits to working remotely, as we've seen in the last few chapters. But there are also big challenges to overcome.

## Organizing Your Home Schedule

One of these challenges has to do with the way you organize your time at home effectively. It's easy to get carried away without a proper routine to follow, and this can be a huge stumbling block to your productivity. When working in an office, your morning commute can help you wake up, and feel ready to work by the time you get to your desk at home. However, the transition from your pillow to your computer can be more of a task in itself. What you need is a remote working toolbox with effective strategies like the ones listed below to help you make better use of your time and maximize productivity:

- **Get Started Right Away on Your To-Do List** - Begin your morning right away with a to-do list. There may be a lot to do, but the key to doing it all is to pace yourself right from the start. Long-distance runners don't exhaust all their energy supply as soon as they leave the starting line. They start at a steady pace and maintain that momentum, so it's enough to sustain themselves until they reach the finish line. Start your morning with your most difficult tasks and slowly work your way through the list progressively. A to-do list is a necessary part of your routine because, without it, it can be easy to dilly dally, taking your time over a prolonged breakfast and before you know it, half the day is gone and you've barely made a dent in your tasks. The morning sluggishness can be the biggest temptation to overcome and it's going to take some self-discipline mentally to get through it.

- **Do Your Most Challenging Tasks in the Morning** - At the start of the day is when we have the most energy and fuel, so start your day with the hardest jobs first. If you've found yourself prone to procrastinating the harder tasks in the past and leaving them to the very last minute, try switching things around and start with the hard stuff first. When you're done with that hard task, move on to smaller, more doable tasks until the end of your workday. Getting the most unpleasant bits of the tasks out of the way first will make the rest of your process a lot more bearable when you think about it. The hardest tasks are the ones we always feel like procrastinating on the most. When you get the hard stuff out of the way, you find you feel much happier, lighter, and things seem more manageable somehow for the rest of the day.

- **Pretend You're Going to the Office -** Behave just as you would if you were going to an office, except this time minus the commute. If it helps you get into the right mindset needed for work and makes you a lot more productive than your pajamas do, maintain the routine you had when you were getting ready to go to the office every day. Wake up in the morning when your alarm rings, change out of your pajamas, make your morning cup of coffee, and prepare to start work as though you were in an office environment. This role-playing might not seem like it's doing much to help, but it's better to pretend than to find yourself in bed all day or struggling to wake up in the mornings and getting nothing done.

- **Simulate the Structure of A Busy Day At The Office** - Structure your day like you would in the office. You are your own boss and personal manager. This is going to help with the challenge that some remote workers face where they end up clocking in more hours than they should. That's why there is a distinct need for separation between work and personal life. Without it, both lives can easily bleed into each other, and you lose out on the work-life balance that was supposed to e a perk of the job. Create to-do lists and calendar reminders for the tasks you need to tackle, the same way you do in an office.

- **Work on A Timer** - Procrastination happens because we become easily distracted from the tasks we're supposed to be doing, and when that happens, we lost track of time. It's not easy for some people to sit down for hours in front of their laptop, typing away and trying to stay focused on work. To overcome this, put yourself on a timer each time you need to get something done. It can be for 30 minutes, an hour, an hour and a half; it is up to you. But for that portion of time, put away all distractions and tell yourself you are going to do nothing but concentrate on work. When your time is up, then allow yourself a break, walk around, check your phone, anything you need to recharge for a moment before getting back to work.

- **Empower Yourself with Positive Beliefs -** Replace your old limiting beliefs with beliefs that are going to empower you moving forward. Get rid of those old thought patterns that made you feel stressed, unproductive, and demotivated in the past and replace them with thoughts that will surge you forward on the path to success. Believe you deserve all that you desire. Believe that you have what it takes to make your dreams come true. You already got to this point where you're not working from home like you always wanted. That shows you have the capability to do anything if you put your mind to it.

- **Make Time for Self-Care** - You don't have to be busy all the time. Being busy doesn't necessarily mean you're productive. Likewise, being productive doesn't mean you need to be busy every minute of the day. Trying to do too much at once is how you clutter your mind and trigger intense, stressful emotions. When you're burned out and worn out, you get even less done so give yourself permission to unwind and relax. This was one of the reasons why you wanted to work from home in the first place. Because you wanted to be able to find balance in your life instead of making it all about work and the stress of trying to do it all. Self-care is as important as getting things done because when your health is compromised, you get nothing done. So make time to go to the gym now that you don't have to commute to work anymore. Make it a point to establish a healthy diet at home now that you don't have the excuse of not having any time or being too tired after you've rushed home from work. All the things you previously did not have time for because you had to commute to work and you were stuck in the office under the watchful eye of many is now a thing of the past now that you're working remotely. Take advantage of that.

- **Gratitude Everyday** - Most of all, make time in your day to be grateful. It's a privilege to live in a time when remote working is possible. Where we can have the best of both worlds. A new habit to develop that keeps your mind organize is to schedule time in your day again to log what you're grateful for. Make it a point to list at least five things you were grateful for today. If you've got more, even better, write them all down. This exercise makes you actively think about the good things happening in your life. That despite the difficult day you might have had, there were still moments of positivity in it that brought a smile to your face. Taking the time to count your blessings is one approach to achieving more balance in your life.

## Greater Clarity Comes With Meditation

Concentration is another big challenge that is faced by many who work from home. There will be some days when you can focus and concentrate better than others, and some days where you struggle to get through a single task. But how will sitting in silence for several minutes a day going to make a difference in the way you work remotely? It can be difficult to see the link between meditation and why it can make a difference to your quality of life and the way that you work, especially when you're working remotely with a lot more distraction challenges on your plate.

There is no doubt the number one benefit that you might say will bring about the biggest difference to your quality of life. Dealing with stress is not as simple as simply avoiding what triggers your stress. Mental and physical stress can come can stem from anywhere. Jobs, finances, friends, and family. These triggers are not exactly something you can avoid forever. Our bodies and minds may be strong and tough, but there is only so much negativity that it can take before it starts to take its toll and affect our health, sometimes to a point where it could become unbearable. That's when it becomes difficult to focus on work. Stress produces cortisol, and when that happens, our memory is impaired, our blood pressure rises, our sleep gets disrupted, and we end up feeling unmotivated and fatigued. Not to mention the fact that cortisol can eventually lead to more severe conditions like anxiety and depression too.

Many of us undergo undue amounts of tension in our everyday life, and sometimes the load can seem unbearable. One way to cope with this is to employ a simple breathing technique that can be utilized when you are under stress:

- *While keeping your mouth closed, breathe in and out through your nose quickly in short cycles but maintaining an equal amount for each breath.*
- *Aim for three in-and-out breath cycles every second, after which you will breathe normally.*
- *In your first attempt, do not do this for more than 15 seconds. You can incrementally by 5 seconds each time you do this exercise until you reach a full minute.*

We can use meditation to change our perception and thoughts in negating these negative energies and begin to fully appreciate and live in the moment. We can begin our process of healing by following the steps below:

- *Find a quiet spot and sit down with your feet firmly on the ground.*
- *As always, breathing and focus are key components in this exercise and I want you to first focus on these two parameters before moving onto the next step.*
- *Once you have achieved a sense of calm and focus, you will need to be aware of your thoughts and emotions.*
- *Also, pay close attention to any signs your body might be making during this*
- *process.*
- *Take your time to understand your emotions and thoughts.*
- *When you're in this state, you will need to remind yourself that just because you made a wrong choice or put faith in the wrong person, doesn't mean that you have to doubt every choice you are going to make in the future. Keep reminding yourself of this.*
- *Focus on respecting your choices as much as you respect the choice of others.*

- *Respect your opinion as much as you respect the opinion of others.*
- *Establish that any choices you make are the best, as nobody knows you better than yourself.*

Being isolated and working by yourself a lot of the time can lead to overthinking and negative thoughts. In order for you to achieve inner peace, you must negate al negative thoughts from consuming you and controlling your emotions. Using meditation, we can use its techniques to provide us with ways to combat negative thoughts: -

- *Sit in a quiet, comfortable space, breathe, relax, and detach away from the rigors of everyday life.*
- *Channel your thoughts and focus on what feels good to your senses. Don't focus on the areas of your body that is in pain or uncomfortable. Realign your focus on areas that feel good.*
- *Think of yourself as an ocean with waves on the surface but calmness and serenity beneath it.*

- *Once you have achieved this state, you are more adept to any stimuli from your surroundings.*
- *Try to hone in and listen more to your surroundings instead of trying to decipher or understand them.*
- *Feel your breath throughout your body. Breathe slowly and feel each breath entering and leaving your body until you achieve a sense of stillness within you.*
- *This is the level that you are trying to achieve, like a calm ocean floor. This is the calmness that you need to achieve every time you need to combat negative energies and thoughts that plague you.*

Meditation is the number one self-improvement habit. If you could install one new habit into your life, it would be meditation. Just a few minutes a day is all you need to bring about incredible changes in your ability to gain clarity, focus, and concentration. The beauty of meditation is that it is simple yet powerful. Simple enough that anyone can learn how to do it effectively with the right tools, teachings, and techniques. Anyone can learn the art of meditation, and it isn't as difficult as you may imagine. Sure, you may have tried it a few times and found yourself struggling in the early stages to quiet your mind and achieve a focus, calm, and mindful state, but that is perfectly normal, especially if you're a beginner just starting out on this journey.

Meditation requires you to reconnect with yourself, mind, body, and soul. It helps you find your focus, feel centered, and feel more connected to your surroundings in a way you've never had before. Finding a quiet spot for you to meditate daily. If you can't manage this daily, meditating several times a week would be good enough to start. Meditation is a great tool to help you feel centered emotionally again, teaching you to practice feelings of calm and learning to let go of all the stress you may have encountered during the day.

An extension of those meditation exercises mentioned above is yoga. Yoga comes with numerous health benefits, among which include improved flexibility, increased muscle strength, an increase in your body's awareness, higher lung capacity and blood circulation through the movements that you're encouraged to do, relaxation of your joints and muscles, even improved levels of concentration, discipline and focus. Unlike cardio and weight training exercises, yoga isn't as demanding because it doesn't place a lot of stress or strain on your body's muscles. It is a different approach to exercising your body, focused on building strength and concentration while simultaneously helping you remain calm. It extends on the quick relaxation exercises by encouraging deeper muscle movements through controlled physical activity. Numerous studies have revealed that yoga could even help to reduce anxiety, which could be an anger trigger for some. When you're feeling anxious all the time, you're highly strung, and even the smallest of incidences could be enough to rub you the wrong way, and things get blown out of proportion.

Yoga requires a quiet spot for you to gain the full benefit of the calming technique. It's also going to require more time commitment, 20-30 minutes of your time if you have that to spare during the day. If you've only got 5-10 minutes of your time to spare, that's perfectly okay too, go with what works for you. Yoga's effective relaxation techniques lie in helping you focus on controlled, slow, and deliberate movements.

## Organizing Your Home Office

Is your home office wall cluttered with all kinds of stuff? It is set up in a way that is going to be comfortable and encourage productivity for several hours a day. Sure, you may have a desk and a chair, but the problem is that desk and chair you're working with *may not be designed for you.* If you spend several hours a day slouching, reaching too far forward or hunched over while you're typing on your computer, it's going to lead to some serious health and posture problems eventually. You need to set up your work station ergonomically to avoid pain in the long-term, and the more comfortable you are, the easier it will be to concentrate on what you have to do instead of being distracted by the aches and pains in your joints.

Aside from being better for your overall health and to minimize injury, ergonomic workspaces improve your productivity. It's easy to stay focused when you're comfortable and not fidgeting left and right, trying to get into a comfortable position. Ergonomic workspaces are more than just making sure you're in a well-lit environment or that your chair is comfortable enough. It involves the way your worktop is positioned and that it is adjusted to a height that promotes good posture for you. Your desk should be at a height that is comfortable enough for you to type and work for a long time if needed, and your chair should be designed to support good posture to avoid any muscle tension or aches and pains from sitting down too long. Here are several other things you can do to set up an ergonomic home office that is designed specifically for you:

- **Adjusting the Height of Your Chair** - The average height of a work desk is between 29 - 30 inches tall. Some people might find this too tall or too short. That's where a good quality chair comes in. You want to start off by adjusting the height of your chair accordingly, and when you do, your elbows should be bent to 90 degrees.

- **Get A Footstool** - If your feet are not touching the floor when you're sitting at your desk, this can quickly become an issue. To resolve this problem, invest in a footstool, and if you don't have one, a ream of paper is going to be a good substitute.

- **Adjust the Height of Your Monitor** - If you're working with a desktop setup, your computer monitor should be positioned at about arm's length and easy to read without straining your eyes. You shouldn't have to bend forward or adjust your posture either to read what is on your screen. Raise the height of your computer monitor until the top of the screen is at eye level. Again, if your monitor is the type that does not have an adjustable height, your reams of paper are going to come in handy once more. Now, if you're working with two computer monitors, you need to consider how you use them. There will be one primary monitor, and this should be the monitor that is right in front of you. If you use both monitors equally, then line them up so *you are in the middle* of both these monitors.

- **Raising Your Laptop Height** - When you're working with a laptop, a kickstand is going to come in handy in raising your laptop to the right height. You can use an external keyboard and mouse since this is going to be the more comfortable option to go with.

- **Positioning Your Keyboard and Mouse** - The area of the table your mouse ends up is where you want your keyboard to be. Your mouse should be right next to your keyboard, allowing you to move from your elbows instead of your shoulders. This will prevent your shoulder muscles from being overused or too strained. The key is you *do not want to be reaching for your tools.*

- **Positioning Your Phone** - If you require a physical phone other than your mobile for work purposes, you want to position your phone on your non-writing side. This means if you write with your right hand, you want to position the phone on your left and vice versa. This setup will prevent the need to cradle your phone against your shoulder, which can lead to serious neck pain down the road if you do it often enough. Alternatively, consider using a headset if you have to be on the phone quite a bit.

- **Light the Area Well** - It can be hard to concentrate when you're squinting and trying to get as close to your screen as possible to make out the words. Natural lighting is the best, although not always possible. If that's the case, opt for ambient lighting to avoid the glare bouncing off your computer screens. When reading documents or books, an adjustable, low-glare lamp works best, so your reading material is always well-lit. Having to re-read sentences multiple times is not conducive to productivity, and the frustration of not being able to see is going to disrupt your ability to focus.

Finally, remember to move around and stretch during the day. We all have a tendency to start slouching in our chairs after 15-minutes or more of sitting there working. Get up from your chair every hour. Walk around, look out the window, stretch your arms, and stretch your legs. Take care of your body and avoid sitting at your desk for long periods of time, even if it is ergonomically set up. Most importantly, set up your home office in such a way that it is suitable *for you* and with minimal distractions. It's a mobile world we live in these days. With more opportunities to work remotely and on the go, there may be times when we find ourselves having to work at different locations. When that happens, setting up your perfect space can be a challenge, but it's still doable. Depending on where you are, make little tweaks and adjustments to your space until you feel comfortably satisfied with the outcome. Angle your computer away from any distractions. Clear the table of any clutter and put it aside temporarily. Put on noise-canceling headphones for better concentration.

## Keeping the Team Spirit Alive

There has never been a better time for remote working than right now. But a genuine concern for many who are about to embark on this journey is that the relationship dynamics between colleagues and leadership might change. It is important to keep that relationship and team spirit alive, especially for a manager, so you don't end up losing control over your employees. Managers need to acknowledge the fact that some of your remote employees may experience work FOMO (Fear of Missing Out) since they're not around as much as their on-site colleagues. Working with others in an inevitable part of the job, even when you're a remote worker.

Being a leader is not easy. The demands and the constantly changing environment makes you feel like you can never let your guard down. That you always need to be on your toes. Not only are you responsible for your work, but you are also responsible for inspiring, leading, and motivating a team of individuals under you to be the very best that they can be every day at work to achieve the set goals. If your team is a ship, you (as the leader) are its captain, and the successful navigation of that ship depends on how well you do at the helm. Juggling the different relationship dynamics within that team successfully so everyone can work as a cohesive unit. As the leader, an important part of your job is going to be ensuring that *all members of your team,* whether onsite or remote, feel a sense of camaraderie and are comfortable working with each other. To ensure the continuity of strong relationships even among remote employees, you'll need to:

- **Put in Some Effort** - Working remotely is not easy. It does require a certain temperament and skills to succeed, but these skills can be learned. The leader needs to make a deliberate effort to reach out regularly and encourage members of your team to do the same with each other. Relationships don't happen overnight, even when you're working on site. In a remote working setting, building relationships means having to rely on the proper channels to do so. Encourage your team to carry on personal conversations virtually to help maintain some normalcy and lessen the isolation that they feel. Let them know it's okay if they want to talk about something other than work.

- **Use Tech and Collaborative Tools to Your Advantage** - In the office, several types of conversations take place, and it's a good idea to create the right channels for these conversations to happen so all your team members can be a part of it. If you're using Slack, for example, you could create channels for work and for fun.

- **Encourage Accessibility** - It's not just the team leader that should be accessible. Everyone should. Encouraging video calls (not always to talk about work) can really put a name to a face so your people don't feel like they're only talking through email or chat rooms, which can at times still lack the personal, human touch. Seeing the different people, you're working with at least once a week, even if it is through video, can build trust among coworkers.

- **Don't Worry About Over-Communicating** - This scenario is a lot better than lacking communication. There is no such thing as over-communicating when it comes to remote employees. It's good communication. Encourage your remote team to reach out to you whenever they face a roadblock or find certain tasks challenging. Written communication is great, but it is prone to misinterpretation, especially when you're giving advice or trying to encourage someone.

## Major Software Tools You Need In Your Remote Working Toolbox

Work is better when you've got the right tools on your side, supporting your every need. As you prepare to make the transition into life as a remote employee or the leader of a remote working team, these are some of the tools you want to consider:

- **Slack** - Some companies are perfectly happy using Skype or Skype Instant Messaging, but if you want to take it a step further, then Slack is one option to consider. It brings together applications, data, and people. Slack replaces the function of an email in your company. There's a massive flow of information and communication happening in a company daily, and emails are only one part of it. Getting 20 to 50 work emails a day might be overwhelming to some, and if you're in a hurry, something might get overlooked. Slack turns inboxes into messages and organizes those messages into channels. All members of the team on that channel will instantly see any updates that get posted, increasing the return on communication. It changes the communication dynamic from being individually focused to now a team focused one.

- **Zoom** - It is essentially simplistic and powerful video conferencing software. It quickly replaced Skype and FaceTime as the popular video calling tool in 2020 when many people were forced to work from home. Online meetings, conferences, and even virtual schools are easy with Zoom.

- **Monday.com** - Another software that helps you thrive in a remote setting is Monday.com. Weekly schedules are among this platform's best features. Working remotely, it is critical to know who is working on what days and on what documents and Monday makes it easy to track that. Users can also communicate changes in shifts in a section for updates. Meetings and recaps also make it easy for your team to stay in the know, no matter where or which time zone they are in. there is also a handy little location column, so you know where your team members are all the time.

- **Remo Conference** - This is another platform for hosting virtual events. It's easy to navigate, and it has segmented roundtable sessions that will instantly connect you to a shared video chat.

- **MeetFox -** Yet another video conferencing tool that will allow you to coordinate your meetings run your video conferences, and even send invoices with minimal effort. If you're looking for an all-in-one packaged deal, this is a pretty good consideration to explore.

- **Process Street** - One of the best no-code workflow management tools out there. Think of this as a super-powered checklist, if you will. Easily walk your team through recurring processes. Automate your workflow easily, prioritize tasks, and make it easy for your team to follow well-written processes with no problem.

- **Google Drive** - Mentioned here once again, Google Drive is by far the safest place for your file storage and management needs. Store files, documents, pictures, spreadsheets, presentations, and more.

- **1Password** - Never have to worry about your team forgetting or losing access to important passwords needed to access certain company material again. Since several of your employees sometimes need access to the same login information, make it easier for them and you by storing passwords in secure software like 1Password.

If you want to find these lists updated and just a click away, visit the website:

https://www.lineprofile.net

or go directly to the living book page:

https://www.lineprofile.net/remote-teams/

Living Books Insights is the formula that allows you to obtain additional information on the subject matter, continuous updates, further comments, withdraw your bonuses and above all to have all the links mentioned in the book and others at your fingertips, as well as an updated review of the main tools available on the market.

# Conclusion

Thank you for making it through to the end of *Working Remotely*, let's hope it was informative and able to provide you with all of the tools you need to achieve your goals whatever they may be.

If you're thinking about making the transition to full-time remote work, hopefully, this book has inspired you that it is going to be a decision you won't regret. If you're already remote working, you're way ahead of the curve, and hopefully, you have found the information in this book useful to improving your current work from home system. Either way, remote working is the perfect solution to attain the work-life balance that many employees these days so eagerly want. There is nothing quite like the freedom and flexibility of setting your own schedule, working at your own pace and style, working from the comfort of your home or wherever in the world you may be, *and* being paid to do it.

Regardless of company shape and size, remote working employees are steadily growing every year. With new technology and software emerging all the time to support this need for remote work efficiency, it's safe to say that one day, office spaces might be a thing of the past and no longer a necessity. Better productivity, greater levels of staff happiness, more motivation, reduced stress, there's no reason why we would ever want to go back to the old way of spending hours in rush hour traffic and battling the stress of getting to work on time when there's a much, much better option on our hands. Thousands, and possibly millions of employees today have already discovered what a joy it is to be working from home. Isn't it time you were one of them?

Finally, if you found this book useful in any way, a review on Amazon is always appreciated!